Basic Cookbook for Kids Ages 5-8

Table of Contents

Table of Contents 2
Disclaimer 8
How to Handle Kids in the Kitchen 9
    Kitchen Safety Tips 9
    Tools and Measurements 11
    Reading a Recipe 12
    Maintaining Cleanliness in the Kitchen and Staying Organized 14
Breakfast Recipes 16
    Animal Face Toast 16
    Berry Orange Chia Pudding 19
    Overnight Oats 21
    Yogurt Parfaits 23
    Chocolate Peanut Butter Balls 25
    Devil Face Devilled Eggs 28
    Toast with Strawberries and Honey 31
    Cottage Cheese Breakfast Toast 33
    French Toast Mugs 35
    Spinach Egg Muffins 38
    Cheesy Ham and Hash Brown Casserole 40
Lunch Recipes 43
    Colorful Pinwheel Wrap 43
    Chicken Salad Sandwiches 45
    Salad with Mixed Greens, Lentils, & Apple 47

Tomato & Avocado Sandwich 49
Bacon Pea Salad 51
Mac n Cheese 53
Meat Wrap 55
California Melt 57
Crispy Quesadillas 59
Peanut Butter and Jelly Sandwich 62
Turkey Wraps 64

Grocery List 67

Dinner Recipes 68
Italian Deli Wraps 68
Black Bean Quinoa Bowl 70
Red Sauce Pasta 72
Pita Pizza 75
Antipasto Pinwheel Sandwich 77
Corned Beef Sandwiches 80
Sheet Pan Chicken and Cauliflower 81
Baked Cod and Vegetables 85
Refried Bean Burrito 88
Grilled Turkey Sandwich 92
Chicken Nuggets 94

Snacks and Desserts 97

- Cheesy Nachos 97
- Banana Roll-ups 99
- Chickpea Snack Salad 101
- Crunch Mix 102
- Peanut Butter Granola Pinwheels 104
- Almond Joy Balls 106
- Antipasto Kabobs 108
- Rainbow Fruit Skewers 110
- Caprese Salad Skewers 112
- Fruity Peanut Butter Pitas 114
- Nutella Quesadillas 115
- S'more Pops 118
- Yogurt and Berry Popsicles 120
- Raspberry-Pistachio Greek Yogurt Bark 122
- Avocado Banana Chocolate Pudding 124
- Princess Toast 126
- Rice Cake Funny Faces 128
- Stuffed Dates 130
- Glazed Doughnut Holes 131
- No Bake Cereal Bars 133
- Watermelon Split 136

Healthy Smoothies and Drinks 139

- Pineapple and Banana Smoothie 139
- Peanut Butter Avocado Smoothie 141

Chocolate Banana Smoothie 143

Carrot and Orange Smoothie 144

Teddy Bear Smoothie Bowl 146

Berry Banana Smoothie Bowls 148

Oreo Milkshake 151

Mango Julius 152

Virgin Mojito Mocktail 154

Chocolate Milkshake 156

Ocean Water Punch 157

Holiday and Party Recipes 160

Christmas Bark 160

Eggs in a Basket 163

Reindeer Sandwiches 165

Ground Beef Tacos 167

Mini Burgers 171

Magic Wands 173

Pigs in a Blanket 175

Birthday Cake Freezer Pops 177

Marshmallow Pops 180

Peach Crisp Parfait Popsicles 182

Pizza Pasta Skewers 184

Ricotta, Blueberry, and Grape Toasts 187

Fun Cooking Activities *190*

Breakfast Charcuterie Board 190

Reindeer Bites 193

Party Charcuterie Board 196

Monster Mash Potato 198

Pancake Time 201

Eggs in a Nest (Spaghetti and Meatball Muffin Bites) 205

Frosted Sugar Cookies 207

Thumbprint Cookies 212

Owl Toast 216

Banana Muffins 218

Sleeping Bag Blondies 221

Bonus Recipes *226*

Healthy Oatmeal Muffins 226

Fruit and Granola Yogurt Bowl 228

Bacon Cream Cheese Pinwheels 231

Chocolate Chia Pudding 233

Chickpea & Quinoa Grain Bowls 235

Sweet Potato & Bean Quesadillas 237

Avocado, Tomato & Chicken Sandwich 239

Roast Chicken & Sweet Potato 241

Steak Bites & Mushrooms 243

Sweet Potato Smoothie Bowl 245

Turkey Apple Cheddar Sandwich 248

Black Bean and Sweet Potato Salad 249

Flying Saucers 252

Frozen Banana Cereal Pops 253

Quick Taco Wraps 255

Kitchen Dictionary *258*

Recipe Journal *261*

Conclusion *262*

Disclaimer

Copyright © 2025

All Rights Reserved.

No part of this eBook can be transmitted or reproduced in any form including print, electronic, photocopying, scanning, mechanical or recording without prior written permission from the author.

While the author has taken utmost efforts to ensure the accuracy of the written content, all readers are advised to follow information mentioned herein at their own risk. The author cannot be held responsible for any personal or commercial damage caused by information. All readers are encouraged to seek professional advice when needed.

As this is a kids book, adults are needed to be present at all times to ensure kids are able to complete tasks and recipes with safety.

How to Handle Kids in the Kitchen

Regardless of age, cooking is an activity that anyone can enjoy. Cooking is not just about food. It's an interactive process that teaches you a lot about the food you eat and makes you aware of where it comes from and the effort that goes into it. This book is perfect if you want to introduce your little one to the world of cooking. With a little guidance and supervision, your little one can whip up delicious dishes in no time. This can be an excellent bonding activity, too.

Before beginning, here are some basics of cooking your little one must know.

Kitchen Safety Tips

Children need supervision, and this is true for their time in the kitchen, too. Here are some safety tips your child must know before entering the kitchen and cooking.

- The most important rule is that your child must know they should ask an adult before doing anything. Whether it is handling ingredients, kitchen tools, or an appliance, ensure they ask.
- Along the same lines, ensuring children are always under adult supervision when in the kitchen is important. Whether it's parents or a caregiver, ensure your child is not left by themselves in the kitchen, especially when they are 5-8 years old.
- Teach about maintaining hand hygiene. This means that children must thoroughly wash their hands with soap and water before cooking and after touching certain ingredients, such as eggs and raw meat.
- Encourage them to wear appropriate clothing while cooking, such as short-sleeved cotton clothes. If they have long hair, ensure it is tied up.
- Teach them awareness about hot surfaces such as wearing oven mitts or potholders while handling dishes coming out of the oven or a hot pan.
- Knives and other shop tools in the kitchen must be used only under adult supervision.

- Give age-appropriate tasks. Whether it is washing and peeling vegetables, stirring, or measuring ingredients, ensure the tasks in the kitchen are age appropriate.

Tools and Measurements

Before you introduce your children to cooking, it's important that you have the right tools in place. Can you paint without brushes and other art supplies? Similarly, ensure you have kid-friendly kitchen tools.

These days, a variety of choices are available when it comes to children-friendly kitchen tools. Choosing the right ones ensures your child's cooking experience is easy and fun. One key point to consider while selecting kitchen tools is to look for simple designs. Whether it is knives, measuring cups, or spoons, look for ones in bright colors with large and easy-to-read marking. Since safety is always important, opt for a small blunt knife or a plastic knife and a small peeler with a protective guard for your child in the kitchen. Look for mixing bowls and kitchen utensils that are colorful to make cooking fun. Another consideration is to avoid utensils that are heavy or made of glass.

Here are some basic kitchen tools your child will need.

- Keep a set of plastic and kid-friendly knives in the kitchen. Don't let them use sharp knives without your supervision.
- Two mixing bowls, one medium and one large.
- Different measuring cups are needed, but the most commonly used ones are marked as 1 cup, 1/2 cup, 1/3 cup, and 1/4 cup.
- Similarly, you'll need to keep a few measuring spoons marked as one tablespoon and one teaspoon.
- Apart from measuring tools, other basic kitchen tools needed for cooking are a whisk, chopping board, spatula, peeler, apron, oven mitts, and tongs.

Reading a Recipe

An important aspect of encouraging children to Cook is helping them read a recipe. This entirely depends on your child's reading level. For 5–8-year-olds, reading a recipe might be a little tricky, but with your help, it will become easy. It's not just about reading the words but understanding what they mean as well.

Reading the recipe is an important practice, especially before you start cooking. The recipe lists out the ingredients to be used, their quantities, and the steps to be followed. In this book, you will find a variety of recipes ideal for 5–8-year-olds in the kitchen. A simple practice is to ensure your child goes through the recipe before they begin. While reading the recipe, encourage them to gather the required ingredients. Once the ingredients are in place, check the quantities and help them measure it out. All this prep must be in place before the actual cooking begins. Doing this not only teaches them about kitchen etiquette but helps them understand the importance of being organized while cooking as well.

Encourage your child to read the recipe by themselves. Help if they struggle. While reading, ask them what each line of the recipe means. This ensures they understand the steps properly. You can also ask them to identify the ingredients to make things more interesting.

Maintaining Cleanliness in the Kitchen and Staying Organized

Apart from kitchen safety, it's important to teach children about maintaining cleanliness in the kitchen and staying organized. Here are some simple tips you can use.

- Be a good role model for them in the kitchen. By demonstrating appropriate kitchen behavior, you set a good example for the children to follow.
- Teach them to keep things in their designated places. For instance, if they remove the chopping board from its place, ensure they keep it back after use.
- To stay organized, encourage children to clean up as they cook. For instance, after peeling fruits or vegetables, the scraps must be thrown in the bin and shouldn't be left on the countertop.
- Similarly, ensure they not only help with cooking but cleaning too. This is not only important but a great way to teach them responsibility too.
- Keep meat and animal foods away from fresh produce. This prevents cross-contamination. For instance, if a certain chopping board is used for meat, ensure that produce such as vegetables and fruits are handled on another one.

Now, we've covered a lot so far in understanding the basics of cooking, kitchen safety and kitchen tools. We've summarized all of that information into a single page so you can print it out and stick it on the kitchen wall for you and your child to keep referencing. Just scan the QR code below to get the sheet.

Breakfast Recipes

Animal Face Toast

Put a fun twist on breakfast by turning regular toast into cute animal faces with simple toppings!

Level: Easy

Serves: 4

Preparation time: 5 minutes

Cooking time: 3 – 4 minutes

Nutritional values per serving: 1 toast

Calories: 263

Fat: 10 g

Carbohydrates: 42 g

Protein: 7 g

Ingredients:

- 4 slices of sandwich bread
- a little whipped cream
- 4 small bananas
- 8 fresh blueberries
- 3 – 4 strawberries
- 4 tablespoons peanut butter or any other nut/seed butter

Directions:

1. Cut the bananas into desired shapes, like circles or semi-circles. The circles can be used for eyes. 2 semi-circles can be placed such that they resemble lips, leaving a slight gap between them.

2. Cut the strawberries into the desired shape. You can cut into strips or along the length of the strawberries. The blueberries can be used as eyes or pupils of the eyes.

3. Place the bread slices in the toaster and toast them to the desired crunchiness.

4. place the bread slices on a tray or individual serving plates.

5. Spread a tablespoon of the nut butter over each toast. You can use different butters for different toasts. You can use chocolate spread for the monkey's face. Use whipped cream where white is required, but make sure to spread it over the nut butter layer.

6. Next, place the banana slices for the eyes (owl and monkey). Place blueberries to make the eyes or pupils.

7. The strawberry strips can be used to make whiskers.

8. You can make the nose either with banana or strawberry slices. The slices can be used to make ears as well. You can use your own imagination or ask the kids to use their creativity to make different animals. I have only given suggestions of a few animal faces.

9. Serve once the faces are made.

Berry Orange Chia Pudding

You teach them how to pour the ingredients into a bowl, add the berries and chia seeds, and stir.

Level: Easy

Serves: 2

Preparation time: 2 minutes plus chilling time

Cooking time: 0 minutes

Total time: 2 minutes plus chilling time

Nutritional values per serving: 1 bowl

Calories: 188

Fat: 9 g

Carbohydrates: 26 g

Protein: 4 g

Ingredients:

- 7 ounces of canned coconut milk
- ¼ cup orange juice
- 1 tablespoon pure maple syrup
- ½ cup mixed berries
- ¼ cup chia seeds

Directions:

1. Pour orange juice, maple syrup, and coconut milk into a blender. Drop the berries into the blender and blend until very smooth.
2. Pour into an airtight container. Add chia seeds and stir. Let it rest for 15 minutes. Stir every 5 minutes.
3. Cover the container and chill overnight.
4. Stir and divide the pudding into two bowls.
5. Serve.

Tip: You can replace coconut milk with any other milk.

Overnight Oats

You will teach the kids to mix up ingredients by stirring. Allow them to choose the toppings (preferably anything colorful and crunchy) and place them over the oats.

Level: Easy

Serves: 2

Preparation time: 5 minutes plus chilling time

Cooking time: 0 minutes

Nutritional values per serving: 1 bowl, without toppings and optional ingredients

Calories: 272

Fat: 8 g

Carbohydrates: 38 g

Protein: 11 g

Ingredients:

- 1 cup old-fashioned rolled oats
- ½ cup plain Greek yogurt or milk
- 1 cup milk of choice
- 4 teaspoons maple syrup or honey
- 1 teaspoon vanilla extract
- 2 teaspoons chia seeds (optional)
- 1/8 teaspoon sea salt
- toppings of your choice like granola, nuts, etc. (optional)

For the add-ins: Optional

- 2 tablespoons peanut butter or strawberry jam or jam of your choice
- 4 tablespoons chocolate chips
- ½ cup fresh chopped fruit or berries

Directions:

1. Take a lidded container and place chia seeds and oats in it.

2. Pour in the milk, vanilla extract, maple syrup, and yogurt. Add the salt as well and stir the mixture.

3. If you want to add any optional add-ins now, stir well.

4. Cover the container and chill overnight in the refrigerator. It can be stored for about 3 – 4 days.

5. Stir well once again just before serving.

6. Spoon the oats into two bowls. Place the toppings and serve.

Yogurt Parfaits

They will learn to layer the ingredients and build a parfait. It will teach them portion control as they scoop and place the ingredients in the jar. They can use their creativity to build a parfait of their choice.

Level: Easy

Serves: 2

Preparation time: 10 minutes

Cooking time: 0 minutes

Nutritional values per serving: 1 jar

Calories: 338

Fat: 16 g

Carbohydrates: 36 g

Protein: 14 g

Ingredients:

- 1 cup plain whole milk yogurt
- 2 tablespoons hemp seeds or chia seeds or shredded unsweetened coconut
- ½ cup fresh or frozen, thawed berries or chopped mangoes, applesauce or chia jam or berry jam, etc.
- ½ cup crunchy topping like granola or crunchy cereal, mini animal crackers or puffed cereal, etc.

Directions:

1. Scoop ¼ cup of yogurt and place in a Mason's jar.
2. Scatter ¼ cups of fruit over the yogurt. Scoop out ¼ cups of yogurt and place it over the fruits.
3. Sprinkle a tablespoon of hemp seeds.
4. Scatter ¼ cup of crunchy topping on top and serve.
5. Make the other parfait similarly or layer as per your choice.

Chocolate Peanut Butter Balls

It takes a little elbow grease to mix the ingredients (you should do it), so you can teach them how to make the balls and measure the ingredients.

Level: Medium

Serves: 12

Preparation time: 10 minutes

Cooking time: 0 minutes

Nutritional values per serving: 1 ball

Calories: 114

Fat: 6 g

Carbohydrates: 8 g

Protein: 6 g

Ingredients:

- ¾ cup old-fashioned rolled oats
- 2 tablespoons honey or maple syrup
- 1 tablespoon chocolate chips
- ½ cup natural peanut butter
- 1 scoop of chocolate protein powder

Directions:

1. Measure the oats, protein powder, honey, peanut butter, and chocolate chips and add into a mixing bowl. Keep stirring until well incorporated.

2. If the mixture is very dry, crumbling, and not coming together, add a teaspoonful of water or almond milk at a time and mix well each time until the dough comes together. You may need to use your hands to mix the dough.

3. Scoop out the mixture using a small cookie scoop and place it on a plate lined with parchment paper.

4. Now, pick up each dough and shape it into balls. Place the balls in an airtight container. They can be chilled in the refrigerator or frozen.

Devil Face Devilled Eggs

Teach the kids how to peel boiled eggs, mash the yolks, fill the egg cavities, and decorate the eggs like devils. The older kids can also be taught to boil the eggs.

Level: Easy

Serves: 3

Preparation time: 20 minutes

Cooking time: 10 minutes

Nutritional values per serving: 1 egg (2 egg halves)

Calories: 120

Fat: 10 g

Carbohydrates: 1 g

Protein: 6 g

Ingredients:

- 3 eggs
- 1 teaspoon Dijon mustard

- a tiny pinch of paprika
- 1 ½ tablespoons mayonnaise
- ½ teaspoon white wine vinegar
- a pinch of freshly ground pepper
- a pinch of salt
- 2 green bell pepper strips (½ inch wide)
- 2 red bell pepper strips (½ inch wide)
- 1 sprig of fresh dill
- 1 fresh chive

Directions:

1. Chop each bell pepper strip into six triangles. So you have 12 triangles each of red and green bell peppers. Cut the chives into 12 pieces and the dill into smaller six sprigs.

2. Gently place the eggs, one at a time, in a saucepan. Add water to the saucepan, ensuring the water level is at least 2 inches over the eggs.

3. Put the saucepan over high heat. Let it come to a boil. Let it boil rapidly for 2 – 3 minutes. Turn off the heat and place a lid on the saucepan to cover completely. Set it aside.

4. After 10 – 12 minutes, drain the water and fill the saucepan with cold water. After about 5 minutes, drain the water again and peel the eggs.

5. Cut each egg into two halves lengthwise. Put them on a plate.

6. Using a small spoon, scoop the yolks from the egg halves and place them in a bowl.

7. Add the seasonings, vinegar, mustard, and mayonnaise to the bowl of yolks. Mash the yolks with a fork.

8. Take a piping bag and fix it with a large tip. Spoon the yolk mixture into the piping bag and pipe the yolks into the cavities of the egg whites. If you do not have a piping bag, you can use a small spoon to fill the cavities with the yolk mixture.

9. Make horns of the devil using two red pepper triangles on each egg half. The fangs can be made by using two green bell pepper triangles on each. The eyes can be made using two pieces of chives. The moustache can be made using the dill sprig. And lo, the little devils are ready to serve. They can also be served chilled.

Toast with Strawberries and Honey

You teach them how to spread yogurt or other foods like butter, nut butter, jam, etc. Older kids can be taught to toast the bread slices too. Also, let them decorate the toast with strawberry slices using their creativity.

Level: Easy

Serves: 2

Preparation time: 5 minutes

Cooking time: 2 – 3 minutes

Nutritional values per serving: 2 toasts

Calories: 255

Fat: 3 g

Carbohydrates: 50 g

Protein: 12 g

Ingredients:

- 4 slices whole-grain bread
- 2 cups strawberry slices
- 8 tablespoons vanilla Greek yogurt
- 2 teaspoon honey

Directions:

1. Mix the bread slices into the toaster and toast them with the desired crunchiness.
2. Place the bread slices on a large plate. After cooling the toast for a couple of minutes, smear two tablespoons of Greek yoghurt on each toast.

3. Decorate with strawberry slices. Trickle honey over the toasts and serve.

Cottage Cheese Breakfast Toast

You teach the kids how to spread cottage cheese and nut butter. Older kids can be taught to toast the bread slices. You can also let them decorate the toast with berries.

Level: Easy

Serves: 2

Preparation time: 5 minutes

Cooking time: 3 – 4 minutes

Nutritional values per serving: 1 toast

Calories: 249

Fat: 12 g

Carbohydrates: 25 g

Protein: 13 g

Ingredients:

- 2 slices sprouted bread or any other of your choice
- 2 tablespoons almond butter
- ½ cup low-fat cottage cheese
- ½ cup mixed berries of your choice

Directions:

1. Drop the bread slices into the toaster and toast them with the desired crunchiness.
2. First, spread a tablespoon of almond butter over each toast. Spread a thick layer of cottage cheese (using four tablespoons) over each toast.
3. Decorate with berries and serve.

French Toast Mugs

Even a 5-year-old can make this French toast without messing up their hands. You can teach them how to tear the bread and stir the ingredients in a mug. Older kids can be taught how to break an egg.

Level: Easy

Serves: 2

Preparation time: 5 minutes

Cooking time: 1 minute

Nutritional values per serving: 1 mug, without toppings

Calories: 238.3

Fat: 10 g

Carbohydrates: 22.1 g

Protein: 10.3 g

Ingredients:

- 2 teaspoons butter
- 2 teaspoons maple syrup
- ½ teaspoon vanilla extract
- 2 large eggs
- 3 – 5 bread slices (enough to make 2 cups)
- 6 tablespoons whole milk
- ½ teaspoon ground cinnamon
- 1/8 teaspoon ground nutmeg

Directions:

1. Tear the bread slices into bite-size pieces.
2. Add a teaspoon of butter into two large microwave-safe mugs3. Melt the butter in the microwave for about 15-18 seconds.
3. Add a teaspoon of maple syrup, ¼ teaspoon of vanilla extract, ¼ teaspoon of cinnamon, and a pinch of nutmeg into each mug.

4. Add three tablespoons of milk into each mug. Crack an egg into each mug.

5. Whisk the ingredients well Using a small hand whisk or a fork.

6. Drop a cup of bread pieces into each mug and stir until the bread is coated with the mixture. Make sure the bread pieces do not break into smaller pieces.

7. Cook on high power in the microwave for about 90 seconds or until no liquid remains in the mugs and the mixture is well cooked.

8. Serve with toppings. The toppings could include berries, nuts, chocolate chips, banana slices, syrup, or peanut butter.

Spinach Egg Muffins

This recipe is a nice way to introduce greens to your kids while explaining their benefits. Teach them to grease the muffin cups, whisk the ingredients, and pour them into the muffin cups.

Level: Easy

Serves: 6

Preparation time: 10 minutes

Cooking time: 20 minutes

Nutritional values per serving: 1 muffin

Calories: 87

Fat: 6 g

Carbohydrates: 1 g

Protein: 7 g

Ingredients:

- 4 eggs
- 1 cup finely chopped baby spinach

- ½ teaspoon garlic powder
- ½ cup shredded cheddar cheese
- 2 tablespoons Greek yogurt
- ¼ cup finely chopped red bell pepper
- ¼ teaspoon dried oregano
- a pinch of salt
- a pinch of pepper

Directions:

1. Set the oven temperature to 350° F and allow it to preheat.
2. Meanwhile, spray a 12-count muffin pan with some cooking oil spray or grease with oil using a silicone brush. Be generous with the oil. If you own a silicone pan, that would be great. Use that to make the muffins.
3. Crack the eggs into a bowl and whisk until well combined. Add Greek yogurt, salt, pepper, oregano, and garlic powder and whisk well.

4. Stir in the spinach, bell pepper, and cheese.

5. Spoon the mixture into the muffin cups. Make sure all the cups have almost the same quantity of the mixture.

6. Place the muffin pan in the oven and bake until the muffins are set but not jiggle.

7. Cool for a few minutes before removing them from the pan.

8. Serve.

Cheesy Ham and Hash Brown Casserole

Let the kids learn to mix the ingredients and spread them in a casserole dish. They can also spread the cheese. Older kids can be taught to grease the dish with cooking oil.

Level: Easy

Serves: 6

Preparation time: 15 minutes

Cooking time: 50-60 minutes

Nutritional values per serving: 1/6 recipe

Calories: 415

Fat: 27 g

Carbohydrates: 30 g

Protein: 14 g

Ingredients:

- 1 package (16 ounces) frozen hash brown potatoes
- 8 ounces sour cream
- 4 ounces cooked, diced ham
- 1 can (10.5 ounces) condensed cream of potato soup
- 1 cup shredded sharp cheddar cheese
- ¾ cup grated parmesan cheese

Directions:

1. Preheat the oven to 375° F. Prepare a baking dish by greasing it with some cooking oil spray or brushing some oil.

2. Place hash browns in a bowl. Add potato soup, cheddar cheese, sour cream, and ham.

3. Spoon the mixture into the baking dish. Scatter parmesan cheese on top and place it in the oven for about 50-60 minutes or until light brown on top.

4. Serve warm.

Lunch Recipes

Colorful Pinwheel Wrap

This recipe is filled with colorful vegetables. Teach kids the benefits of different vegetables. Let them layer the sandwich as they wish (spreading and placing vegetables).

Level: Easy

Serves: 2

Preparation time: 5 minutes

Cooking time: 0 minutes

Nutritional values per serving: 1 sandwich

Calories: 233

Fat: 12 g

Carbohydrates: 19 g

Protein: 13 g

Ingredients:

- 2 large soft tortillas
- ½ cup cucumber strips
- ½ cup carrot strips
- ½ cup red or yellow bell pepper strips
- 8 tablespoons hummus

Directions:

1. Cut the carrot, bell pepper, and cucumber into matchsticks.
2. Place a tortilla on a large plate. Take out four tablespoons of hummus and spread it evenly over the tortilla.
3. Scatter the vegetables (¼ cup each) all over the tortilla.
4. Roll the tortilla tightly from the end closest to you, right up to the other end, and place the wrap with its seam side facing down. Preferably wrap in cling wrap and place in the

refrigerator for a while. These can last for about 2 days in the refrigerator.

5. Repeat the process with the other tortilla as well.
6. Cut the wrap into about 1-inch wide pinwheels and serve.

Chicken Salad Sandwiches

You can teach them how to mix the ingredients and prepare a sandwich.

Level: Easy

Serves: 2

Preparation time: 10 minutes

Cooking time: 0 minutes

Nutritional value per serving: 1 sandwich

Calories: 430

Fat: 19 g

Carbohydrates: 27 g

Protein: 19 g

Ingredients:

- ¾ cup cooked, chopped chicken
- ½ small onion, finely chopped
- 1/8 teaspoon salt
- 4 slices bread
- ¼ cup chopped celery rib
- ¼ cup mayonnaise or salad dressing
- 1/8 teaspoon pepper or to taste

Directions:

1. Combine the chicken, onion, salt, celery, mayonnaise, and pepper in a bowl. Taste it and add more seasonings if necessary.

2. Divide the salad among two slices of bread. Spread the salad all over the bread slices. Cover with the remaining bread slices. Cut into the desired shape and serve.

Tip: You can replace chicken with turkey or chopped boiled egg. Of course, the nutritional value will change.

Salad with Mixed Greens, Lentils, & Apple

This is a nice way to introduce salads to kids. Explain the importance of eating fresh salads. You can also teach them how to build a salad.

Level: Easy

Serves: 2

Preparation time: 10 minutes

Cooking time: 0 minutes

Nutritional values per serving: 1 plate

Calories: 347

Fat: 13 g

Carbohydrates: 48 g

Protein: 13 g

Ingredients:

- 3 cups mixed salad greens
- 2 apples, cored, sliced, divided
- 2 tablespoons red wine vinegar
- 1 cup cooked or canned, drained lentils
- 3 tablespoons crumbled feta cheese
- 4 teaspoons extra-virgin olive oil

Directions:

1. Take two serving plates. Spread 1 ½ cups of the greens on each of the plates. Scatter ½ cup of lentils over the greens.

2. Place ¼ of the apple slices over the lentils on each plate. Scatter 1 ½ tablespoons of feta cheese over the apple slices.

3. Drizzle two teaspoons of oil and one tablespoon of vinegar over each salad.

4. Place remaining apple slices alongside and serve. This way, they will eat the apple as it is and learn to eat it on the salad with dressing.

Tomato & Avocado Sandwich

While making this sandwich, you teach the kids to mash, spread, and assemble the sandwich. Older children can be taught how to scoop and mash an avocado.

Level: Easy

Serves: 1

Preparation time: 10 minutes

Cooking time: 0 minutes

Nutritional values per serving: 1 sandwich

Calories: 278

Fat: 11 g

Carbohydrates: 35 g

Protein: 11 g

Ingredients:

- ¼ medium, ripe avocado, peeled, pitted, mashed
- ½ medium tomato, cut into round slices
- 2 tablespoons hummus
- 2 slices whole-wheat bread
- 1 tablespoon finely chopped shallot

Directions:

1. Toast the bread slices to the desired crispiness. Smear the mashed avocado on one toast. Place tomato and shallot on the avocado layer.
2. Smear hummus over the other toast and place on the tomato layer with the hummus side down.
3. Cut into the desired shape and serve.

Bacon Pea Salad

Teach your kids to toss a salad. Older kids can be taught how to grate cheese as well.

Level: Easy

Serves: 2

Preparation time: 10 minutes

Cooking time: 0 minutes

Nutritional values per serving: ¾ cup

Calories: 218

Fat: 14 g

Carbohydrates: 14 g

Protein: 9 g

Ingredients:

- 2 cups frozen peas, thawed
- ¼ cup ranch salad dressing
- salt and pepper to taste
- 2 bacon strips, cooked, crumbled
- ¼ cup shredded sharp cheddar cheese
- 1 small red onion, chopped

Directions:

1. Mix well with peas, dressing, seasonings, cheese, and onion in a bowl.
2. Cover the bowl and place it in the refrigerator for 45 – 60 minutes.
3. Add bacon and stir. Divide into two plates and serve.

Mac n Cheese

Teach your kids to make mac and cheese by themselves. They can measure the ingredients and place them in individual mugs for cooking.

Level: Easy

Serves: 2

Preparation time: 2 – 3 minutes

Cooking time: 5 minutes

Nutritional values per serving: 1 mug

Calories: 380

Fat: 15 g

Carbohydrates: 40 g

Protein: 21 g

Ingredients:

- 2/3 cup dry, uncooked elbow pasta
- 2/3 cup water
- 1 cup finely shredded cheese
- pinch of salt
- 2/3 cup milk

Directions:

1. Take two large, wide, microwave-safe mugs and place 1/3 cup of pasta in each mug.
2. Add a pinch of salt and 1/3 cup of water into each mug. Place the mugs in the microwave and cook on high power for 4 minutes, stirring the mixture after every minute.
3. When no more water is in the mugs, add 1/3 cup of milk and ½ cup of cheese into each mug.
4. Put the mugs back in the microwave and cook for another minute.
5. Stir well. Serve after cooling for a few minutes.

Meat Wrap

Teach your kids how to assemble the ingredients in a wrap and then roll. Let them layer the ingredients as per their liking.

Level: Easy

Serves: 2

Preparation time: 10 minutes

Cooking time: 1 minute

Nutritional values per serving: 1 wrap

Calories: 699

Fat: 36 g

Carbohydrates: 53 g

Protein: 43 g

Ingredients:

- 2 flour tortillas (10 inches each)
- ½ cup shredded cheddar-Monterey Jack cheese blend
- 1 cup chopped tomatoes
- 8 black olives
- 8 slices roast beef
- 1 cup shredded lettuce
- ½ cup chopped onion
- 4 tablespoons Italian-style salad dressing

Directions:

1. Take two microwave-safe serving plates and place a tortilla on each.
2. Place four slices of roast beef, spreading it all over each tortilla.
3. Sprinkle ¼ cup of cheese over the beef on each tortilla.
4. Cook the tortillas in the microwave, one at a time, for about 40 – 50 seconds until the cheese melts.
5. Scatter ½ cup of lettuce, ¼ cup of onion, ½ cup of tomatoes, and four olives on each tortilla.

6. Drizzle two tablespoons of salad dressing on each.

7. Starting from the side nearest to you, roll the tortilla along with the filling and place with its seam side down.

8. Serve.

California Melt

Teach your kids how to assemble a sandwich. You can either instruct them as per the recipe or let them get creative with the ingredients.

Level: Easy

Serves: 2

Preparation time: 15 minutes

Cooking time: 5 minutes

Nutritional values per serving: 1 open-faced sandwich

Calories: 335

Fat: 23 g

Carbohydrates: 21 g

Protein: 16 g

Ingredients:

- 2 slices whole-grain bread
- ½ cup sliced mushrooms
- 4 tomato slices
- ½ avocado peeled, pitted, sliced
- 3 tablespoons roasted, sliced almonds
- 2 slices Swiss cheese

Directions:

1. Set the oven to broil mode and preheat.
2. lightly toast the bread slices and place them on a baking sheet.
3. Distribute the avocado, almond, mushroom, and tomato slices equally and place them over the toasted bread slices.

4. Place a slice of cheese on top of each sandwich and pop the baking sheet into the oven. Once the cheese melts, take it out of the oven.

5. Cool for a couple of minutes and serve.

Crispy Quesadillas

This recipe teaches kids how to make a quesadilla (filling, folding, etc.). They can do the entire thing themselves except baking. Let them choose and place the toppings as per their preference.

Level: Easy

Serves: 2

Preparation time: 5 minutes

Cooking time: 15 minutes

Nutritional values per serving: 1 quesadilla, without toppings

Calories: 735

Fat: 40.5 g

Carbohydrates: 41.3 g

Protein: 49.9 g

Ingredients:

- ½ tablespoon avocado oil or any cooking oil
- 6 ounces shredded Mexican cheese
- 2 flour tortillas (12 inches each)
- 1 ½ cups shredded, cooked chicken

For toppings:

- salsa
- sour cream
- shredded lettuce
- shredded cheese
- olives
- diced tomatoes
- pico de gallo

- any other toppings of your choice

Directions:

1. Set the oven temperature to 425° F and allow it to preheat.
2. Grease a baking sheet using some of the oil.
3. Lay one tortilla on one end of the baking sheet.
4. Spread 1/3 cup of cheese on half the tortilla. Layer ¾ cups of chicken over the cheese. Spread 1/3 cup of cheese over the chicken layer.
5. Lift the other half of the tortilla and fold it over the filling. Make sure the edges of the tortilla are together. It doesn't matter if the edges do not touch each other.
6. Keep the other tortilla in the remaining space. Repeat the steps 4 and 5.
7. Brush the remaining oil on top of the tortillas.

8. Place the baking sheet in the oven for about 6 minutes. Take it out and turn the quesadillas over. Continue baking until they turn crisp and golden.

9. Slice into wedges and place the chosen toppings before serving.

Tip: You can use any other filling instead of chicken, such as mock meat, refried beans, shredded beef, crumbled tofu, or steak.

Peanut Butter and Jelly Sandwich

Let the kids learn to make this all-time favorite sandwich. They will learn how to spread the ingredients over bread slices.

Level: Easy

Serves: 4

Preparation time: 2 – 3 minutes

Cooking time: 0 minutes

Nutritional values per serving: 1 sandwich

Calories: 358.4

Fat: 17.8 g

Carbohydrates: 41.4 g

Protein: 11.9 g

Ingredients:

- 4 slices sandwich bread
- 4 teaspoons grape jelly or strawberry jam
- 4 tablespoons creamy or crunchy peanut butter

Directions:

1. Take two tablespoons of peanut butter and smear it on one slice of bread.
2. Spread two teaspoons of jelly or jam on another slice of bread.
3. Now place the slice with jam over the slice with peanut butter with the jam side facing down to complete the

sandwich. Cut into the desired shape and serve. Repeat the steps and make the other sandwich similarly.

Turkey Wraps

Use this recipe to teach your kids how to fill a wrap and roll them up.

Level: Easy

Serves: 3

Preparation time: 20 minutes

Cooking time: 0 minutes

Nutritional values per serving: 1 wrap

Calories: 524

Fat: 38 g

Carbohydrates: 20 g

Protein: 25 g

Ingredients:

For the spread:

- 4 ounces cream cheese at room temperature
- ¼ cup fresh basil leaves
- 2 tablespoons mayonnaise

For the wraps:

- 3 tortillas (12 inches each)
- 3 slices cooked bacon
- 1/8 cup thinly sliced red onion
- 3 lettuce leaves
- ½ pound sliced, cooked turkey
- 3 slices cheddar cheese
- 1 cup microgreens

Directions:

1. Whisk the cream cheese and mayonnaise in a bowl using an electric hand mixer.

2. Add in the basil leaves and give short pulses until the basil is well combined with the cream cheese mixture.

3. To make the wraps: Place a tortilla on a plate and spread 1/3 of the cream cheese mixture all over the tortilla.

4. Place 1/3 of the turkey slices over the tortilla, leaving about 1-inch around the edges.

5. Place a slice of bacon, a little of the onion, a lettuce leaf, and 1/3 cup of microgreens on the edge closest to you. Place one cheese slice over the filling.

6. Now roll the tortilla along with the filling right up to the other end and place it with its seam side facing down. Wrap it in cling wrap.

7. Repeat the process with the other two tortillas (steps 3-6).

8. Chill the wraps for about a couple of hours.

9. Unwrap and cut into slices. Serve. Tip: You can use any other meat or spread instead of the one in the recipe.

Grocery List

I hope you're enjoying the recipes. If you'd like a grocery list of all the items you need to cook the recipes in this book, just scan the QR code below to get it.

Dinner Recipes

Italian Deli Wraps

Teach your children how fun layering and wrapping can be.

Level: Easy

Serves: 1

Preparation time: 5 – 6 minutes

Cooking time: 0 minutes

Nutritional values per serving: 1 wrap

Calories: 778.5

Fat: 57.8 g

Carbohydrates: 27 g

Protein: 37.7 g

Ingredients:

- 2 teaspoons butter at room temperature
- 2 slices provolone cheese
- 2 slices bologna
- 2 slices deli ham
- 1 flour tortilla (10 inches)
- 10 slices pepperoni
- 3 slices tomatoes
- 2 teaspoons mayonnaise
- 6 banana pepper rings (optional)
- 2 lettuce leaves

Directions:

1. Smear butter over the tortilla.

2. Make sure you do not place any filling along the edges of the tortilla. Place cheese slices over the tortilla. Next, place ham slices followed by bologna.

3. Place the pepperoni slices over the bologna, followed by banana peppers, if using.

4. Next, place the tomato slices followed by lettuce. Smear the mayonnaise over the lettuce.

5. Start from the side closest to you and start rolling tightly up to the opposite end.

6. You can serve it right away or refrigerate it for about 2 hours wrapped in cling wrap.

Black Bean Quinoa Bowl

Teach them how to make a dressing and mix the ingredients. Let them build the bowl as well.

Level: Easy

Serves: 2

Preparation time: 10 minutes

Cooking time: 0 minutes

Nutritional values per serving: 1 bowl

Calories: 500

Fat: 16 g

Carbohydrates: 74 g

Protein: 20 g

Ingredients:

- 1 ½ cups canned or cooked black beans, rinsed, drained
- ½ cup hummus
- ½ medium avocado, peeled, pitted, diced
- ¼ cup chopped fresh cilantro
- 1 1/3 cups cooked quinoa
- 2 tablespoons lime juice
- 6 tablespoons Pico de Gallo

Directions:

1. Add beans and quinoa into a bowl and stir. Divide the mixture into two bowls.

2. Combine lime juice and hummus in a bowl to make the dressing. Add enough water to dilute the hummus.

3. Pour dressing on top of each bowl. Scatter avocado and cilantro on top. Place three tablespoons of Pico de Gallo in each bowl and serve.

Red Sauce Pasta

Children love pasta. This is an easy recipe for kids to follow. Make them measure out the ingredients and follow the steps. The only thing you need to do is operate the microwave for them.

Level: Easy

Serves: 2

Preparation time: 10 minutes

Cooking time: 10 minutes

Nutritional values per serving: 1 bowl

Calories: 765

Fat: 23 g

Carbohydrates: 113 g

Protein: 25 g

Ingredients:

- 2 cups dry, uncooked elbow pasta
- ½ teaspoon salt or to taste
- 2 tablespoons olive oil
- 4 tablespoons tomato sauce
- 2 tablespoons shredded mozzarella cheese
- 2 teaspoons dried Italian herbs
- 1/8 cup sliced black olives
- 2 cups water

- 1 tablespoon finely chopped garlic
- ½ cup milk
- ½ cup cherry tomatoes, halved
- 1 tablespoon grated parmesan cheese
- 2 teaspoons chopped chives or green onion

Directions:

1. Measure out the pasta and water and add into a microwave-safe bowl. Add salt and olives and stir well.

2. Cook on high power in the microwave for 5 – 8 minutes, stirring every minute or so, until the pasta turns nearly al dente.

3. Stir in tomato sauce, milk, cherry tomatoes, cheese, Italian herbs (you can use oregano, basil, etc.; you can also use mixed dried herbs), and cheese.

4. Taste some of the sauce and adjust the salt and seasonings if required. Continue cooking in the microwave for 2 – 3 minutes until nice and hot.

5. Distribute the pasta into two bowls and serve.

Pita Pizza

Let them use their creativity and decorate the pizza with toppings they like. They can make funny faces on their pizzas too. Each pizza can be decorated differently.

Level: Easy

Serves: 6

Preparation time: 10 minutes

Cooking time: 10 minutes

Nutritional values per serving: ½ pizza

Calories: 158

Fat: 6 g

Carbohydrates: 20 g

Protein: 8 g

Ingredients:

- 3 pita breads
- ½ can (from a 4 ounce can) of sliced black olives, drained
- 1 small tomato, cut into thin slices
- 2 ounces blue cheese, crumbled
- 1/8 teaspoon dried oregano
- 1/8 teaspoon dried basil
- 1/8 teaspoon crushed coriander seeds (optional)
- 3.5 ounces tomato sauce
- ½ ounce diced pimento peppers, drained
- 2 ounces shredded mozzarella cheese

Directions:

1. Set the oven temperature to 425° F and allow it to preheat.
2. Heat the pita bread in a microwave for 50 – 60 seconds.
3. Place the pita bread on a large baking sheet. Spread some of the tomato sauce on each pita. Press the pita as you spread.

4. Decorate the pita with olives, tomatoes, pimento peppers, seasonings, mozzarella, and blue cheese. You can scatter cheese first and place the other toppings over it or the other way around.

5. Bake until the pizza is cooked as per your preference.

6. Cut each into two halves and serve.

Antipasto Pinwheel Sandwich

Another great recipe to teach your kids how to layer and assemble a sandwich.

Level: Easy

Serves: 4

Preparation time: 15 minutes plus chilling time

Cooking time: 0 minutes

Nutritional values per serving: ½ sandwich

Calories: 399

Fat: 29 g

Carbohydrates: 17 g

Protein: 20 g

Ingredients:

- 2.6 ounces cream cheese, softened
- 2 whole wheat tortillas (8 inches each)
- 3 tablespoons thinly sliced fresh basil
- 1 ½ tablespoons sun-dried tomato pesto
- 3 tablespoons canned, sliced pepperoncini peppers, drained (optional)
- 10 slices salami

Directions:

1. Blend the sun-dried tomato pesto and cream cheese in a bowl. Make sure it is well combined. You can also use it on a mini food processor or an electric hand mixer.

2. Place the tortillas on plates. Smear the cream cheese mixture all over the tortillas, including the edges. Retain a little of the mixture.

3. First, scatter the pepperoncini all over the tortillas, followed by basil. Do not scatter on one of the edges (about 1 ½ inches).

4. Lay five salami slices on each tortilla over the basil and pepperoncini.

5. Start rolling the tortillas tightly from the salami side up to the opposite side. Use the retained cream cheese mixture to seal. Wrap them individually in cling wrap and chill for at least 2 hours and up to 48 hours.

6. Unwrap just before serving. Cut into two halves and serve.

Corned Beef Sandwiches

Let the kids learn the art of spreading and building the sandwiches.

Level: Easy

Serves: 2

Preparation time: 5 minutes

Cooking time: 0 minutes

Nutritional values per serving: 1 sandwich

Calories: 443

Fat: 17 g

Carbohydrates: 45 g

Protein: 28 g

Ingredients:

- ¼ cup Russian salad dressing
- ½ pound thinly sliced corned beef
- 4 slices rye bread

- 4 ounces of prepared coleslaw

Directions:

1. Spread two tablespoons of Russian salad dressing on 2 of the bread slices and place them on a plate.

2. Place half the corned beef slices over each of these two bread slices.

3. Spread half the coleslaw over the beef.

4. Cover each with a slice of bread. Cut the sandwiches into the desired shape and serve.

Sheet Pan Chicken and Cauliflower

Teach your kids to break a cauliflower into florets and arrange the ingredients on a sheet pan. You can introduce them to different spices. Older kids can be taught to coat the chicken with a spice mixture.

Level: Easy

Serves: 2

Preparation time: 20 minutes plus marinating time

Cooking time: 30 minutes

Nutritional values per serving: 1 plate

Calories: 583

Fat: 39 g

Carbohydrates: 14 g

Protein: 47 g

Ingredients:

For the chicken:

- 3 chicken thighs, boneless, skinless
- ½ teaspoon turmeric powder
- ½ teaspoon ground cumin
- ½ tablespoon ground ginger

- ½ teaspoon paprika (optional)
- ¼ teaspoon ground cinnamon
- 2 cloves garlic, minced
- ¼ cup olive oil

For the cauliflower:

- 1 ½ tablespoons olive oil
- ½ large cauliflower or a small cauliflower
- 1 teaspoon garlic powder

To serve: Optional

- chopped fresh dill or parsley
- thinly sliced red onion

Directions:

1. Set the oven temperature to 400° F and allow it to preheat.

2. While the oven is preheating, prepare the chicken: Measure the ground spices and add them to a bowl. Add in the garlic and oil and stir the mixture until well incorporated.

3. Add chicken and stir well so the chicken pieces are well coated with the spice mixture.

4. Set the bowl aside to marinate for 30 – 60 minutes or slightly longer if you have the time.

5. While the chicken is marinating, prepare the cauliflower: Combine oil and garlic powder in a bowl.

6. Brush a little oil over a baking sheet with a silicone brush or spray some cooking oil.

7. Add cauliflower to the bowl of oil mixture and mix well. Make sure the garlic oil mixture coats the cauliflower well.

8. Scatter the cauliflower pieces towards the centre of the baking sheet. Place the chicken thighs over the cauliflower so that the cauliflower is covered with the chicken. Drizzle any spice mixture from the chicken or cauliflower all over the chicken and cauliflower.

9. Bake until the chicken is cooked through. Distribute the chicken and cauliflower evenly onto two plates.

10. Sprinkle herbs and red onion on top and serve.

Baked Cod and Vegetables

Let the kids learn to arrange the cod and vegetables on a sheet pan. Teach them to line the sheet pan as well.

Level: Easy

Serves: 2

Preparation time: 10 minutes

Cooking time: 35 minutes

Nutritional values per serving: 1 plate

Calories: 330

Fat: 11.4 g

Carbohydrates: 35.5 g

Protein: 24.5 g

Ingredients:

- 1 ½ tablespoons olive oil, divided
- 1 bell pepper of any color, deseeded, chopped into ½ inch pieces
- 2 cloves garlic, minced
- ½ pound baby potatoes, halved
- 1 cup cherry tomatoes
- 2 cod filets (4 – 6 ounces each)
- salt to taste
- pepper to taste
- ¼ teaspoon paprika (optional)
- a handful of chopped parsley, cilantro, or dill, or use a mixture of these
- ½ large lemon, cut into thin slices

Directions:

1. Set the oven temperature to 400° F and allow it to preheat.
2. Take a sheet of parchment paper and place it on a baking sheet.
3. Dry the cod filets by patting them with paper towels.
4. Place the cod filets on a plate. Brush ½ tablespoon of oil on top of the filets. Sprinkle salt, pepper, and paprika.
5. Set it aside for now.
6. Place potatoes on the baking sheet. Drizzle ½ tablespoon of oil over the potatoes and season with some salt. Spread it slightly on the sheet.
7. Place the baking sheet in the oven and bake for about 15 minutes.
8. Move the potatoes onto any side of the baking sheet. Place bell pepper, garlic, and cherry tomatoes on the other side. Drizzle the remaining oil over these vegetables and mix well.

9. Now combine the vegetables and the potatoes and spread them all over the baking sheet. Make sure to make two cavities on the baking sheet (with no vegetables) to place the cod in the cavities.

10. Now, place lemon slices on the cod and the vegetables and continue baking until the cod flakes easily when pierced with a fork.

11. Divide the vegetables into two plates. Place a cod filet on each plate.

12. Garnish with chopped, fresh herbs and serve.

Refried Bean Burrito

Show the kids how to build a burrito. Older kids can be taught how to fold the tortilla into a burrito too. You can teach them to grease the baking dish.

Level: Easy

Serves: 3

Preparation time: 20 minutes

Cooking time: 25 minutes

Nutritional values per serving: 1 burrito, without toppings

Calories: 659

Fat: 26 g

Carbohydrates: 74 g

Protein: 31 g

Ingredients:

- ½ pound lean ground beef
- ¾ cup refried beans or drained, rinsed, cooked or canned black beans
- 1 ½ cups cooked rice
- ¾ cup shredded cheddar cheese
- ½ packet (from a 1 ounce packet) of taco seasoning mix
- 6 tablespoons corn kernels

- 3 large flour tortillas (10 inches each)

For toppings: Optional

- finely chopped red onion
- finely chopped lettuce
- sour cream
- finely chopped fresh cilantro
- diced tomatoes
- salsa
- chopped avocado
- guacamole
- any other toppings of your choice

Directions:

1. Let the oven preheat to 350° F.
2. Grease a square or rectangular baking dish with oil or cooking oil spray.
3. Add beef into a pan and cook over medium heat until it is not pink anymore. As you stir, break the meat into crumbles.

Add taco seasoning and mix well. Stir on and off for about 2 minutes, and take the pan off the heat.

4. Make the burritos one at a time: Place a tortilla over a plate. Place ¼ cups of beans in the centre of the tortilla and spread them around a little but not all over the tortilla. Spread ½ cups of rice over the beans, followed by 1/3 of the beef. Scatter 2 tablespoons of corn and ¼ cup of cheese.

5. Take two opposite sides of the tortilla and fold them inwards over the filling. Start rolling from any one of the other ends right up to the other end, and place it with its seam side facing down in the greased baking dish.

6. Repeat the process (steps 4 and 5) and make the remaining two burritos similarly.

7. Cover the dish with foil and place it in the oven for 20 -30 minutes or until well heated.

8. Serve with any of the toppings if desired.

Grilled Turkey Sandwich

Let your kids learn how to layer and build a sandwich.

Level: Easy

Serves: 1

Preparation time: 5 minutes

Cooking time: 3 – 4 minutes

Nutritional values per serving: 1 sandwich

Calories: 458

Fat: 23 g

Carbohydrates: 36 g

Protein: 28 g

Ingredients:

- 4 tablespoons hummus
- 2 ounces thinly sliced deli turkey
- 1 slice pepper Jack cheese

- 2 slices whole-wheat bread
- 2 tomato slices
- 2 teaspoons butter, softened

Directions:

1. Place a slice of bread on a plate and spread hummus.
2. Place turkey slices over the hummus layer. Next, place tomato slices followed by the cheese slice.
3. Cover with the other slice of bread. Now spread one teaspoon of butter on top of the sandwich.
4. Place a skillet over medium heat. Place the sandwich with the buttered side down when the pan is hot. Now spread the remaining butter on top of the sandwich.
5. Cook until the sandwich is golden brown on either side.

Chicken Nuggets

Teach the kids to bread the chicken pieces. Let them grease the baking sheet by brushing it with oil or spraying it with cooking spray.

Level: Easy

Serves: 3

Preparation time: 20 minutes

Cooking time: 20 minutes

Nutritional values per serving: 1 plate

Calories: 308

Fat: 19 g

Carbohydrates: 15 g

Protein: 9 g

Ingredients:

- 3 skinless, boneless chicken breast halves, cut into 1 ½ inch pieces
- ¼ cup grated parmesan cheese
- ½ cup Italian seasoned breadcrumbs
- ¼ cup butter, melted
- ½ teaspoon salt
- ½ teaspoon dried thyme
- ½ tablespoon dried basil

Directions:

1. The oven is to be preheated to 400° F.
2. Combine breadcrumbs, salt, parmesan, and dried herbs in a bowl.
3. Working with one chicken piece at a time, dip it in melted butter. Lift it and wait 2 – 3 seconds for the excess butter to

drip. Next, dredge the piece in the breadcrumb mixture and place it on the prepared baking sheet. Make sure the chicken pieces do not overlap.

4. When all the nuggets are breaded, bake for about 20 minutes or until the chicken is cooked from the inside and brown on the outside.

5. Serve with a dipping sauce.

Snacks and Desserts

Cheesy Nachos

Who doesn't love nachos? Kids can prepare this recipe by themselves. Tell them how to place the nachos in a single layer without any overlapping. They can spread the cheese themselves too.

Level: Easy

Serves: 1

Preparation time: 5 minutes

Cooking time: 1 minute

Nutritional values per serving: 1 plate without sour cream.

Calories: 158.2

Fat: 10.5 g

Carbohydrates: 7 g

Protein: 8.9 g

Ingredients:

- 3 tablespoons mild taco sauce like Ortega
- 1 cup nacho chips
- black olive slices to garnish (optional)
- 6 tablespoons shredded cheese of your preference
- sour cream to dip (optional)

Directions:

1. Place the chips on a microwave-safe plate.
2. Trickle sauce all over the chips. Adding extra or using less sauce is up to you.
3. Scatter cheese all over the chips. Place olive slices in different spots if you are using them.
4. Place the plate in a microwave and cook on high for 30 seconds or until the cheese has melted.
5. Serve sour cream on the side if desired.

Banana Roll-ups

Teach them how to place the ingredients and folding the tortillas to make banana roll-ups.

Level: Easy

Serves: 2

Preparation time: 10 - 12 minutes

Cooking time: 0 minutes

Nutritional values per serving:

Calories: 443

Fat: 14.1 g

Carbohydrates: 72.3 g

Protein: 11.9 g

Ingredients:

- 2 whole-wheat tortillas
- 2 bananas, peeled (leave it whole)
- ½ cup pretzels
- 1 stalk celery, cut into pieces (optional)
- 2 tablespoons peanut butter
- 8 strawberries, sliced

Directions:

1. Spread a tablespoon of peanut butter on each tortilla. Place a banana along the diameter of a tortilla. Do this with the other banana and tortilla as well.
2. Fold the bottom edge of the tortilla over the banana. Next, fold the sides inwards from the ends of the banana.
3. Start rolling until you reach the other end. This is similar to folding a burrito.
4. Serve this with strawberry, celery, and pretzels.

Chickpea Snack Salad

Teach your kids how combining simple ingredients can result in a delicious salad.

Level: Easy

Serves: 2

Preparation time: 5 minutes

Cooking time: 0 minutes

Nutritional values per serving: 1 bowl

Calories: 202

Fat: 11 g

Carbohydrates: 20 g

Protein: 6 g

Ingredients:

- ½ cup cooked or canned, rinsed, drained chickpeas
- 4 olives pitted, sliced
- ½ cup halved grape tomatoes
- 2 tablespoons red wine vinaigrette

Directions:

1. Add chickpeas, olives, and tomatoes into a bowl and stir until well combined.
2. Pour the dressing over the ingredients in the bowl and stir until well combined.
3. Divide the salad into two bowls and serve.

Crunch Mix

You need not teach them anything about this recipe. Read the instructions and they will happily do it all by themselves. You can teach younger kids to measure the ingredients.

Level: Easy

Serves: 6

Preparation time: 5 minutes

Cooking time: 0 minutes

Nutritional values per serving: ½ cup

Calories: 266

Fat: 14 g

Carbohydrates: 33 g

Protein: 6 g

Ingredients:

- ½ cup plain or frosted animal crackers
- ½ cup miniature pretzels
- ½ cup M&M's
- ½ cup bear-shaped crackers

- ½ cup salted peanuts
- ½ cup chocolate-covered or yogurt-covered raisins

Directions:

1. Toss well with animal crackers, mini pretzels, M&M's, bear-shaped crackers, peanuts, and chocolate-covered raisins in a bowl.
2. Pour the contents of the bowl into an airtight container and store at room temperature.

Peanut Butter Granola Pinwheels

Teach your kids to spread the peanut butter and sprinkle the granola to make delicious pinwheel rolls.

Level: Easy

Serves: 8

Preparation time: 5 minutes

Cooking time: 0 minutes

Nutritional values per serving: 1 pinwheel

Calories: 60

Fat: 3 g

Carbohydrates: 7 g

Protein: 2 g

Ingredients:

- 1 flour tortilla (8 inches)
- ¼ cup granola without raisins
- 2 tablespoons creamy peanut butter
- 1 teaspoon honey

Directions:

1. Place the tortilla over a plate and smear peanut butter.
2. Trickle honey over the tortilla. Scatter granola all over the tortilla. Start rolling tightly, the tortilla from the end closest

to you and place with its seam side facing down. Cut into 1-inch pieces and serve.

Almond Joy Balls

Teach your kids how to measure the ingredients and mix them. Help them with the mixing if needed and turn them into delicious energy balls.

Level: Medium

Serves: 12

Preparation time: 15 minutes

Cooking time: 0 minutes

Nutritional values per serving: 1 ball

Calories: 91

Fat: 6.5 g

Carbohydrates: 8.3 g

Protein: 3.4 g

Ingredients:

- ¾ cup old-fashioned rolled oats
- 2 tablespoons honey or maple syrup
- 1 tablespoon unsweetened shredded coconut
- 1 scoop of chocolate protein powder
- ½ cup natural almond butter
- 1/8 cup finely chopped almonds
- 1/8 cup almond milk

Directions:

1. Add the oats, protein powder, shredded coconut, honey, almond butter, almonds, and almond milk into a mixing bowl. Keep stirring until well incorporated.

2. If the mixture is very dry, crumbling, and not coming together, add a teaspoonful of water or extra almond milk at

a time and mix well each time until the dough comes together. You may need to use your hands to mix the dough.

3. Scoop out the mixture using a small cookie scoop, shape it into balls, and place it in an airtight container. The balls can be chilled in the refrigerator or frozen.

Antipasto Kabobs

Teach your kids how to build kabobs using toothpicks or small wooden skewers. Show them how to stack and give them a creative outlet.

Level: Easy

Serves: 20

Preparation time: 25 minutes

Cooking time: 0 minutes

Nutritional values per serving: 1 kabob

Calories: 66

Fat: 5 g

Carbohydrates: 4 g

Protein: 2 g

Ingredients:

- ½ package (from a 9 ounces package) refrigerated cheese tortellini
- 20 large pitted ripe olives
- 20 thin slices of pepperoni
- 20 pimento-stuffed olives
- 6 tablespoons Italian salad dressing
- 10 thin slices of hard salami, halved

Directions:

1. Read the instructions on the tortellini package and cook it.
2. Place the drained, rinsed tortellini in a bowl along with salad dressing and olives. Toss gently.

3. Keep the bowl in the refrigerator for 4 – 8 hours.

4. Drain off all the liquid from the bowl of pasta.

5. Thread the ingredients on toothpicks in whichever manner you please (tortellini, ripe olive, pepperoni, salami, and pimento-stuffed olive). When you fix the pepperoni and salami, make sure you fold them first and then thread.

6. Serve on a serving platter.

Rainbow Fruit Skewers

Let them use their creativity and thread the fruits onto the skewer in any colorful manner they please.

Level: Easy

Serves: 5

Preparation time: 10 minutes

Cooking time: 0 minutes

Nutritional values per serving: 1 skewer

Calories: 129

Fat: 1 g

Carbohydrates: 31 g

Protein: 2 g

Ingredients:

- 6 orange slices
- 6 blackberries
- 6 red grapes
- 6 strawberries
- 6 kiwi slices
- 6 green grapes
- 12 blueberries

Directions:

1. Cut the orange into slices along with the peel. Now, cut each slice into quarters.

2. Take six small wooden skewers. Thread each skewer with 4 quarters of orange, one each of strawberry, kiwi slice, blackberry, red and green grape, and two blueberries in whatever colorful manner you desire.

3. Place them on a serving platter and serve.

Caprese Salad Skewers

Teach them to build easy skewers by stacking different ingredients.

Level: Easy

Serves: 6

Preparation time: 10 minutes

Cooking time: 0 minutes

Nutritional values per serving: 1 skewer

Calories: 44

Fat: 4 g

Carbohydrates: 2 g

Protein: 1 g

Ingredients:

- 12 grape tomatoes
- 12 fresh basil leaves
- 1 teaspoon balsamic vinegar
- 6 small fresh mozzarella cheese balls
- 1 tablespoon olive oil

Directions:

1. Take a small wooden skewer. Insert two tomatoes, a cheese ball, and two basil leaves in whatever colorful manner as desired onto the wooden skewer. Place on a serving platter.
2. Repeat the process with the remaining skewers.
3. Add vinegar and oil into a bowl and whisk well. Trickle this dressing over the skewers and serve.

Fruity Peanut Butter Pitas

Let the kids learn to spread and fill the pita pockets.

Level: Easy

Serves: 4

Preparation time: 5 minutes

Cooking time: 0 minutes

Nutritional values per serving: 1 pita pocket

Calories: 324

Fat: 17 g

Carbohydrates: 36 g

Protein: 12 g

Ingredients:

- ½ cup peanut butter
- 2 whole-wheat pitas, cut into two halves
- 1 medium banana, sliced

- 1 medium apple, cored, thinly sliced
- ¼ teaspoon ground allspice
- ¼ teaspoon ground cinnamon
- ¼ teaspoon ground nutmeg

Directions:

1. Add peanut butter into a bowl along with the spices and stir until well combined.
2. Spread two tablespoons of peanut butter inside each pita pocket. Stuff the pockets with banana and apple slices and serve.

Nutella Quesadillas

Here, the kids will learn to spread different flavored spreads (apart from regular cheese). The older kids can be taught to fry the quesadilla, and the younger ones can bake it. Let them choose their toppings.

Level: Easy

Serves: 2

Preparation time: 2 minutes

Cooking time: 3 minutes

Nutritional values per serving: 1 quesadilla, without toppings

Calories: 202

Fat: 11 g

Carbohydrates: 24 g

Protein: 2 g

Ingredients:

- 1 tablespoon Nutella or any other hazelnut cocoa spread
- 2 mini flour tortillas

Directions:

1. Place a non-stick pan over medium heat. Spray the pan with some cooking oil spray.

2. Take ½ tablespoon of Nutella and spread it on one half of a tortilla.

3. Lift the other half of the tortilla and fold it over at the centre to make a semi-circle.

4. Place the tortilla in the pan and cook until the underside is golden brown. Flip the tortilla over using a spatula and cook the other side as well.

5. When it is golden brown, transfer it onto a plate. Cut it into wedges if desired. Place the desired toppings and serve. The toppings could be anything, such as fresh fruit, ice cream, chocolate syrup, whipped cream, etc.

S'more Pops

In this recipe, kids will learn how to crush, insert, dip, and dredge ingredients.

Level: Easy

Serves: 12

Preparation time: 10 minutes

Cooking time: 5 minutes

Nutritional values per serving: 1 pop

Calories: 42

Fat: 1 g

Carbohydrates: 8 g

Protein: 0 g

Ingredients:

- 2 ounces of milk chocolate candy coating, melted
- 2 whole graham crackers

- 12 large marshmallows
- 12 lollipop sticks

Directions:

1. Place the graham crackers in a re-sealable bag. Press out all the air from the bag and seal the bag. Now place it on your countertop and press the crackers with a rolling pin or a glass until they are crushed. Transfer them into a shallow bowl.
2. Line a plate with wax paper.
3. Pierce 1 lollipop stick in the center of each marshmallow.
4. Working with one marshmallow at a time, lift the stick and dip 2/3 of the marshmallow in melted chocolate candy coating. Lift it slightly above and let the extra chocolate drip off into the bowl.
5. Next, dredge the marshmallow in cracker crumbs. Let the crumbs cover about half of the chocolate-dipped part. Set aside on the prepared plate.

6. Once the chocolate is set, it is ready to serve. It can also be stored in an airtight container.

Yogurt and Berry Popsicles

Let the kids learn to layer to fill the popsicle molds.

Level: Easy

Serves: 4

Preparation time: 10 minutes plus freezing time

Cooking time: 0 minutes

Nutritional values per serving: 1 Popsicle without sugar

Calories: 66

Fat: 1 g

Carbohydrates: 15 g

Protein: 2 g

Ingredients:

- 1 cup fresh berries of your choice
- 1 ½ tablespoons honey
- ½ cup vanilla Greek yogurt or any other flavored yogurt of your choice
- ½ - 1 tablespoon sugar or more to taste (optional)

Directions:

1. Pour honey and yogurt into a bowl and stir until well combined.
2. You can blend the berries in a blender or chop them into small pieces.
3. Make alternate layers of berries and yogurt in Popsicle molds.
4. Place a Popsicle stick in each mold and freeze until ready to serve.

5. Dip the Popsicle mold in warm water for about 20 seconds before serving. Take it out of the mold and serve it right away.

Raspberry-Pistachio Greek Yogurt Bark

Teach the kids to line the baking sheet with parchment paper. They will learn how to combine, spread, drop, and swirl the jam lightly with a blunt knife to make a delicious bark.

Level: Easy

Serves: 16

Preparation time: 10 minutes plus freezing time

Cooking time: 0 minutes

Nutritional values per serving: 1 piece

Calories: 31

Fat: 1 g

Carbohydrates: 3 g

Protein: 2 g

Ingredients:

- 1 ½ cups whole-milk plain Greek yogurt
- ½ teaspoon vanilla extract
- 1/8 cup chopped pistachios
- 1 tablespoon maple syrup or honey
- 1 tablespoon unsweetened raspberry jam

Directions:

1. Add yogurt, vanilla, and maple syrup into a bowl and stir until well combined.//
2. Spoon the yogurt mixture on a rimmed baking sheet lined with parchment paper.
3. Now spread it into a rectangle of about 5 x 8 inches. Drop bits of jam at different spots over the yogurt layer.

4. swirl the jam lightly into the yogurt with a blunt knife. Scatter pistachios on top.

5. Place the baking sheet in the freezer until stiff. Cut into 16 equal pieces and serve.

Avocado Banana Chocolate Pudding

Kids will learn how to peel and slice the bananas and scoop avocados from their shells. They will also learn portion control and how to fill the pudding bowls.

Level: Easy

Serves: 4

Preparation time: 10 minutes plus chilling time

Cooking time: 0 minutes

Nutritional values per serving: 1 bowl, without toppings

Calories: 308

Fat: 17.27 g

Carbohydrates: 45.32 g

Protein: 6.26 g

Ingredients:

- 4 ripe bananas, sliced
- ¾ cup raw cacao powder
- 1 teaspoon pink sea salt
- 2 ripe avocadoes, peeled, pitted chopped
- 2 teaspoons vanilla extract or one vanilla bean; use only seeds

For the toppings: Optional

- fresh berries
- whipped cream

Directions:

1. Place bananas, cacao powder, salt, avocadoes, and vanilla in a food processor or blender and process until smooth. Scrape the sides of the bowl whenever required.

2. Divide the pudding into four dessert bowls or ramekins and chill for at least an hour before serving.

3. It can last for 2 to 3 days in the refrigerator.

Princess Toast

Kids will learn how to spread the jam evenly and they can decorate as they please.

Level: Easy

Serves: 3

Preparation time: 5 minutes

Cooking time: 2 – 3 minutes

Nutritional values per serving: 1 toast

Calories: 465

Fat: 13 g

Carbohydrates: 82 g

Protein: 3 g

Ingredients:

- 3 slices white bread
- ¾ cup buttercream frosting
- 3 teaspoons silver or golden edible glitter
- 3 tablespoons seedless strawberry jam
- 3 tablespoons sprinkles

Directions:

1. Pop the bread slices into a toaster and toast per the desired crunchiness.
2. Spread a tablespoon of strawberry jam over each toast.

3. Spread ¼ cup of buttercream frosting over each toast, over the jam layer.

4. Scatter a teaspoon of edible glitter and a tablespoon of sprinkles over each toast.

5. You can serve as it is or cut into squares or triangles and serve.

Rice Cake Funny Faces

Kids will have fun decorating the rice cakes with funny faces using different toppings.

Level: Easy

Serves: 2

Preparation time: 10 minutes

Cooking time: 0 minutes

Nutritional values per serving: 1 rice cake funny face

Calories: 71

Fat: 1 g

Carbohydrates: 15 g

Protein: 3 g

Ingredients:

- 2 rice cakes
- ¼ teaspoon ground cinnamon (optional)
- 2 tablespoons low-fat plain yogurt
- 1 strawberry, halved
- ½ kiwifruit, cut into round thin slices
- 4 blueberries

Directions:

1. Cut a kiwi slice into two halves. This can be used to make the mouth. The round slices can be used for the eyes, and the blueberry for the pupils.

2. The strawberry can be used for the nose. This is just my idea. You can also cut the fruits into any desired shape and make any kind of funny face.

Stuffed Dates

Kids will learn how to pit and stuff dates and then garnish them with their choice of toppings.

Level: Easy

Serves: 5

Preparation time: 10 minutes

Cooking time: minutes

Nutritional values per serving: 1 stuffed date

Calories: 87

Fat: 2 g

Carbohydrates: 19 g

Protein: 1 g

Ingredients:

- 5 medjool dates
- ½ tablespoon coarsely chopped dark chocolate
- 5 heaping teaspoons of peanut butter or any nut butter of choice
- 1/8 teaspoon sea salt

Directions:

1. Cut a slit along the length of the dates and remove the seed.
2. Fill a heaping teaspoon of peanut butter in each date and place on a plate. Garnish with chopped chocolate and sea salt and serve.

Glazed Doughnut Holes

Teach the kids to line a baking sheet with wax paper. They will learn how to dip the donut holes in the glaze they make.

Level: Easy

Serves: 6

Preparation time: 10 minutes plus setting time

Cooking time: 0 minutes

Nutritional values per serving: 1 glazed donut hole

Calories: 225

Fat: 4 g

Carbohydrates: 49 g

Protein: 1 g

Ingredients:

- 1 cup confectioners' sugar
- 6 donut holes
- 1 ½ - 3 tablespoons frozen grape juice, cranberry juice, or cherry pomegranate juice

Directions:

1. A baking sheet is to be lined with wax paper.

2. Add confectioners' sugar into a bowl. Initially, add 1 ½ tablespoons of the chosen juice and stir. You need a thick glaze.

3. Add more juice if required, ½ tablespoon at a time, and stir well each time.

4. With a spoon, dunk the donut holes in the glaze one at a time. Pick each one up and place it on the prepared baking sheet.

5. Once the glaze is set, it is ready to serve.

No Bake Cereal Bars

Kids will learn to measure out the dry ingredients and toss them together. They will also learn to grease the baking sheet.

Level: Easy

Serves: 12

Preparation time: 15 minutes

Cooking time: 5 – 8 minutes

Nutritional values per serving: 1 bar

Calories: 350

Fat: 18 g

Carbohydrates: 43 g

Protein: 8 g

Ingredients:

- 2 cups toasted oat cereal
- 1 cup dry roasted peanuts
- 1 cup crispy rice cereal
- 1 cup candy-coated milk chocolate pieces like M&M's
- ½ cup white sugar
- ½ teaspoon vanilla extract

- ½ cup light corn syrup
- ¾ cup creamy peanut butter

Directions:

1. Add oats, peanuts, rice, and chocolate into a bowl and toss well.
2. Take a small rimmed baking sheet and grease it with cooking oil spray or brush with oil.
3. Add sugar and corn syrup into a small saucepan and cook the mixture over medium heat. Stir until the sugar dissolves, simultaneously bringing it to a boil. Turn off the heat.
4. Stir in the peanut butter and vanilla extract and pour into the bowl with the cereal mixture.
5. Stir until well incorporated. Spoon the mixture onto the baking sheet. Spread it evenly and press it well. Let it cool for about 30 – 40 minutes.
6. Make six equal-sized bars and serve.

Watermelon Split

Kids will learn how to mash the berries and measure the required ingredients. With your instructions, they can make the sundae themselves.

Level: Easy

Serves: 2

Preparation time: 10 minutes plus resting time

Cooking time: 0 minutes

Nutritional values per serving: 1 sundae

Calories: 186

Fat: 6 g

Carbohydrates: 32 g

Protein: 4 g

Ingredients:

- 1 teaspoon sugar
- 2 scoops strawberry ice cream or any other ice cream of your choice
- 2 cups watermelon cubes
- ½ cup blackberries
- 4 maraschino cherries
- whipped cream to garnish
- 1/8 cup toasted slivered almonds or peanuts

Directions:

1. Place blackberries in a bowl. Sprinkle sugar over the berries. Take a fork and mash the berries. Let the berries rest for 20 minutes.

2. If there is any juice in the bowl of watermelon cubes, add to the berries, but do not add more than 1 ½ - 2 tablespoons. Mix well.

3. To make the sundae: You need two banana split dishes.

4. Take ½ cup of the watermelon cubes and place them in a banana split dish in the shape of an "X." Scoop out the ice cream and place it in the centre of the "X."

5. Spoon 2 tablespoons of mashed blackberries over the ice cream. Place a blob of whipped cream over the berries. Garnish with two cherries and one tablespoon of almonds, and serve.

6. Make the other sundae similarly.

Healthy Smoothies and Drinks

Pineapple and Banana Smoothie

Kids will learn how to break the broccoli into florets and slice the banana using a blunt knife. Let them place the ingredients in the blender jar as well and they can operate it under your supervision.

Level: Easy

Serves: 1

Preparation time: 5 minutes

Cooking time: 0 minutes

Nutritional values per serving: 1 smoothie

Calories: 302

Fat: 4.2 g

Carbohydrates: 60.5 g

Protein: 9.3 g

Ingredients:

- ¼ cup Greek yogurt
- ½ cup chopped broccoli florets
- ½ banana, sliced
- ¼ cup frozen pineapple
- ½ large green apple, cored, unpeeled, cubed
- ¼ cup water
- Ice cubes, as required

Directions:

1. Blow together yogurt, broccoli, banana, pineapple, apple, and water until smooth.
2. Add ice and blend until very chilled.
3. Pour into a glass and serve.

Peanut Butter Avocado Smoothie

Let the kids peel and slice the banana, scoop the avocado, and place the ingredients in the blender. They can make the smoothie initially without cocoa powder and taste it. Then add the cocoa and blend again.

Level: Easy

Serves: 1

Preparation time: 10 minutes

Cooking time: 0 minutes

Nutritional values per serving: 1 smoothie

Calories: 639.5

Fat: 47 g

Carbohydrates: 44 g

Protein: 21.5 g

Ingredients:

- 5 ounces non-dairy milk, unsweetened
- 2 tablespoons peanut butter
- 1 tablespoon maple syrup or honey
- ½ small-medium avocado, pitted, scooped
- ½ small banana, peeled, sliced
- 1 tablespoon cocoa powder (optional)

Directions:

1. First, place the banana and avocado in the blender jar. Pour in the milk and honey. Add cocoa powder if using. Finally, add the peanut butter. Blitz the mixture until well combined and creamy.
2. You can serve it right away or chill for a couple of hours and serve.

Chocolate Banana Smoothie

Let them learn flavor combinations by combining different ingredients. Let them taste a bit of banana and hazelnut spread individually. When the smoothie is ready, let them know how it tastes when flavors are combined. They can try their own flavor combinations, too, like adding some nut butter, jam, jelly, or fruit of their choice.

Level: Easy

Serves: 1

Preparation time: 5 minutes

Cooking time: 0 minutes

Nutritional values per serving: 1 smoothie

Calories: 268

Fat: 6 g

Carbohydrates: 49 g

Protein: 7 g

Ingredients:

- 1 large banana, sliced
- 2 tablespoons low-fat vanilla yogurt
- ¾ cup vanilla soymilk
- ½ tablespoon Nutella
- ½ cup ice cubes

Directions:

1. Drop the ice cubes into the blender. Place the banana slices in the blender. Pour in the vanilla yogurt and soymilk. Add Nutella.
2. Cover the blender and blitz until smooth.
3. Serve right away.

Carrot and Orange Smoothie

Kids will learn to peel an orange, separate the segments, deseed, and remove the peel from the segments if desired. This is a great way to teach them about flavor combinations.

Level: Easy

Serves: 2

Preparation time: 5 minutes

Cooking time: 0 minutes

Nutritional values per serving: 1 small smoothie

Calories: 75

Fat: 1 g

Carbohydrates: 13 g

Protein: 2 g

Ingredients:

- 1 orange, peeled, separated into segments, deseeded
- 1 medium carrot, peeled, grated
- ¼ teaspoon grated fresh ginger

- ½ cup ice cubes
- 1 tablespoon oats
- ½ cup water or more if required

Directions:

1. Blitz together orange, carrot, ginger, ice cubes, and oats in a blender.
2. Add water to dilute and blend until well combined.
3. Serve.

Teddy Bear Smoothie Bowl

Let the kids decorate the smoothie into a teddy bear smoothie bowl using strawberry slices. Older kids can use a piping bag to pipe the melted chocolate.

Level: Easy

Serves: 2

Preparation time: 10 minutes

Cooking time: 0 minutes

Nutritional values per serving: 1 bowl

Calories: 165

Fat: 5.3 g

Carbohydrates: 27.6 g

Protein: 3.3 g

Ingredients:

For smoothie base:

- 1 cup frozen strawberries
- ½ cup vanilla Greek yogurt
- ½ tablespoon honey or maple syrup

For the bear:

- 2 tablespoons chocolate chips, melted

- 4 round strawberry slices (cut the strawberry crosswise)

Directions:

1. Place strawberries, honey, and yogurt in a blender and blend until smooth.

2. Pour into two bowls.

3. Place a round strawberry slice in each bowl, slightly below the center of the bowl, on the smoothie. This is the nose. Cut the other two strawberry slices into two halves and place 2 in each bowl as ears, dipping the cut part slightly in the smoothie.

4. Pour the melted chocolate into a piping bag and pipe the eyes (big round dot) and mouth (semi-circle like a smile) on the smoothie surface. For the nostrils, pipe the chocolate at two spots on the nose (the round strawberry slice).

Berry Banana Smoothie Bowls

Kids will learn to slice bananas with a blunt knife. Let them measure the ingredients and place them in the blender. Under your supervision, let the kids push the blender button to operate it.

Level: Easy

Serves: 2

Preparation time: 5 minutes

Cooking time: 0 minutes

Nutritional values per serving: 1 bowl without toppings

Calories: 161

Fat: 4 g

Carbohydrates: 28 g

Protein: 5 g

Ingredients:

- ½ cup milk of your choice
- ½ cup sliced banana
- ¾ cup frozen strawberries or blueberries or mixed berries

For the toppings: Optional

- granola
- berries of your choice
- hemp seeds
- chopped nuts
- banana slices
- chopped dried fruit
- shredded coconut
- sprinkles
- chocolate chips
- any other toppings of your choice

Directions:

1. Place banana slices and berries in the blender. Pour in the milk. Cover the blender and blend until smooth.
2. Pour an equal quantity of smoothie into two bowls.
3. Decorate with the chosen toppings and serve.

Oreo Milkshake

Let them break the Oreo cookies and play with the flavors by substituting vanilla ice cream with chocolate ice cream. They can also add peanut butter or some syrup of their choice.

Level: Easy

Serves: 1

Preparation time: 5 minutes

Cooking time: 0 minutes

Nutritional values per serving: 1 smoothie

Calories: 693

Fat: 33 g

Carbohydrates: 90 g

Protein: 12 g

Ingredients:

- 1 cup vanilla ice cream
- 4 Oreo cookies for the milkshake plus one cookie to garnish
- ½ cup milk
- ½ tablespoon chocolate sauce

Directions:

1. Break the Oreo cookies and place them in a blender. Add milk, chocolate sauce, and vanilla ice cream and blend until smooth and frothy.
2. Pour into a glass and serve right away.

Mango Julius

Kids will learn to measure the ingredients and place them in the blender. They can replace mango juice with orange juice or any other juice they choose and get a different flavor.

Level: Easy

Serves: 2

Preparation time: 5 minutes

Cooking time: 0 minutes

Nutritional values per serving: 1 smoothie

Calories: 405

Fat: 9 g

Carbohydrates: 77 g

Protein: 5 g

Ingredients:

- 2 cups mango juice
- 4 tablespoons sugar
- 2 scoops vanilla ice cream
- ½ cup milk
- 2 teaspoons pure vanilla extract

- 1 cup ice cubes

Directions:

1. Place ice cubes in a blender. Add mango juice, sugar, vanilla ice cream, milk, and vanilla extract and close the blender. Blitz until the sugar dissolves and the shake is frothy.
2. Pour into two glasses and serve.

Virgin Mojito Mocktail

Let the kids learn to muddle the mint leaves and combine the ingredients to create a refreshing drink at home.

Level: Easy

Serves: 2

Preparation time: 5 minutes

Cooking time: 0 minutes

Nutritional values per serving:

Calories: 57

Fat: 0 g

Carbohydrates: 15 g

Protein: 0 g

Ingredients:

- 20 large mint leaves or 30 small mint leaves
- 4 tablespoons honey simple syrup
- ½ cup ice cubes or more
- 4 tablespoons lime juice
- 20 ounces sparkling water
- lime slices and fresh mint sprigs to garnish

Directions:

1. Put the mint leaves into a small jug. Add lime juice. Muddle the leaves with a muddler or a wooden spoon for about a minute or until well crushed.

2. Stir in honey, simple syrup, and sparkling water.

3. Place ice cubes in 2 glasses. Divide the mojito equally among the glasses.

4. Top with lime slices and mint sprigs and serve.

Chocolate Milkshake

Kids will learn to measure and pour the ingredients into the blender.

Level: Easy

Serves: 1

Preparation time: 5 minutes

Cooking time: minutes

Nutritional values per serving:

Calories: 380

Fat: 14 g

Carbohydrates: 55 g

Protein: 8 g

Ingredients:

- ¼ cup milk
- ½ cup vanilla ice cream
- 1 ½ tablespoons chocolate flavored syrup

Directions:

1. Blend chocolate syrup and milk in a blender until well combined.
2. Blend the ice cream on low speed until well incorporated.
3. Serve.

Ocean Water Punch

Kids will love pouring the ingredients to get a lovely blue, oceanic-colored punch.

Level: Easy

Serves: 1

Preparation time: 2 minutes

Cooking time: 0 minutes

Nutritional values per serving: 1 glass

Calories: 25

Fat: 0 g

Carbohydrates: 6 g

Protein: 0 g

Ingredients:

- 1 can (12 ounces) lemon-lime seltzer water
- 1 teaspoon Torani blue raspberry syrup
- 1 tablespoon Torani coconut syrup
- crushed ice as required

Directions:

1. Combine seltzer water, blue raspberry syrup, and coconut syrup in a bowl with a spout.

2. Pour into a glass filled with crushed ice and serve.

Holiday and Party Recipes

Christmas Bark

Kids will learn to line the baking sheet with parchment paper and decorate the bark. They can also learn to drizzle the melted chocolate.

Level: Easy

Serves: 24

Preparation time: 10 minutes

Cooking time: 10 minutes

Nutritional values per serving: 1 piece

Calories: 236

Fat: 13 g

Carbohydrates: 26 g

Protein: 2 g

Ingredients:

- 5 ounces dark chocolate callets
- 2 ounces white chocolate callets
- 2 ounces milk chocolate callets
- 2 teaspoons peppermint extract

To decorate:

- candy canes
- sprinkles
- M&M's

Directions:

1. Set up a double boiler: Pour 3 – 4 inches of water into a pot and place the pot over medium heat.

2. Place 4 ounces of the dark chocolate in a heatproof bowl that can fit nicely onto the top of the pot. Ensure the water doesn't touch the bowl, so add water accordingly.

3. As the water starts simmering, the chocolate will melt slowly. I do not recommend melting the chocolate in a microwave, as it tends to burn.

4. When the chocolate melts, stir in peppermint extract with a wooden spoon and turn off the heat.

5. Stir in the remaining dark chocolate.

6. Repeat the same melting process with milk and white chocolate. No peppermint extract needs to be added to these two chocolates. Now, place all three double boilers simmering on low heat.

7. Take a sheet of parchment and place it on a baking sheet.

8. Spoon the dark melted chocolate on part of the baking sheet. With a spoon, make a wavy design over the dark chocolate.

9. Trickle the milk and white chocolate at different spots on the dark chocolate.

10. Decorate with candy canes, M&M's, and sprinkles.

11. Chill until the chocolate sets. Break into pieces and serve. The leftover bark can be stored in an airtight container at room temperature or in the refrigerator.

Eggs in a Basket

Kids will learn to cut the bread to make a basket using a cookie cutter. Older kids can be taught to break an egg too.

Level: Easy

Serves: 1

Preparation time: 5 minutes

Cooking time: 5 minutes

Nutritional values per serving: 1 nest

Calories: 204

Fat: 12 g

Carbohydrates: 14 g

Protein: 10 g

Ingredients:

- 1 ½ teaspoons unsalted butter, divided
- 1 large egg
- freshly ground black pepper to taste
- salt to taste
- 1 slice of whole-wheat bread

Directions:

1. Take a cookie cutter (shape of your kid's choice) and cut bread from the middle of the bread slice.
2. Spread one teaspoon of butter on one side of the bread (the cut and the remaining bread slice).
3. Place a small pan over medium heat. Add ½ teaspoon of butter and let it melt.
4. Lay the bread slice (with the hole) in the pan, with the butter side facing the bottom.
5. Crack the egg into a bowl and carefully pour it into the centre of the bread. Cook for a couple of minutes until the bottom is well cooked.

6. Now, lift the bread slice and the egg using a spatula and flip it over. Cook for about 40-50 seconds, then remove it to a plate. Garnish with salt and pepper.

7. Place the cut-out part in the pan and cook for about a minute on each side.

8. Serve it along with the egg basket.

Reindeer Sandwiches

Teach the kids to cut out hearts from the bread slices using a heart-shaped cookie cutter and to assemble the sandwich, too.

Level: Easy

Serves: 1

Preparation time: 10 minutes

Cooking time: 0 minutes

Nutritional values per serving: 1 sandwich

Calories: 216

Fat: 17 g

Carbohydrates: 11 g

Protein: 8 g

Ingredients:

- 2 slices sandwich bread
- 2 small pretzels
- 1 raspberry or blueberry
- 2 tablespoons peanut butter almond butter, sunflower seed butter, or whipped cream cheese
- 2 chocolate chips

Directions:

1. The pretzels are to be used to make the ears. The chocolate chips are for the eyes, and the berry is for the nose.
2. Take a heart-shaped cookie cutter and cut out hearts from each bread slice.

3. Smear the peanut butter on one bread slice. Place the pretzels as ears partly on the bread (one on each rounded part of the heart).

4. Now, place the other heart precisely over the first heart. The pretzel is partly sandwiched between the slices and partly visible as ears.

5. Place the chocolate chips in the eyes and the berry in the nose.

6. Serve.

Ground Beef Tacos

Kids will learn to build tacos with toppings of their choice. Introduce them to the different spices and flavor combinations. Encourage them to taste individual ingredients to understand their flavor profiles.

Level: Easy

Serves: 4

Preparation time: 15 minutes

Cooking time: 10 minutes

Nutritional values per serving: 1 tortilla with meat, without toppings

Calories: 142

Fat: 4 g

Carbohydrates: 13 g

Protein: 14 g

Ingredients:

- ½ tablespoon olive oil
- 1 teaspoon chili powder or to taste
- ¼ teaspoon dried oregano
- ¼ teaspoon salt
- 1 teaspoon ground cumin
- ¼ teaspoon garlic powder
- ¼ teaspoon black pepper
- ¼ cup water
- ½ pound lean ground beef
- 1 tablespoon tomato paste
- 4 corn or flour tortillas

To serve:

- finely chopped lettuce

- chopped tomatoes
- shredded cheese of your choice
- chopped red onions
- sour cream
- salsa
- any other toppings of your choice

Directions:

1. Cook beef in a pan with oil until brown. Pour off any fat from the pan.
2. Stir in the spices, salt, water, and tomato paste. Cook on medium heat until the mixture is thick. Take the pan off the heat and let it cool until warm.
3. Place ¼ of the meat on each tortilla. Place the desired toppings over the meat and serve.

Mini Burgers

Let the kids cut the bread into circles with a cookie cutter. You can also teach them how to shape burger patties.

Level: Easy

Serves: 6

Preparation time: 20 minutes

Cooking time: 5 minutes

Nutritional values per serving: 1 mini burger

Calories: 68

Fat: 3 g

Carbohydrates: 5 g

Protein: 4 g

Ingredients:

- 2 ounces ground beef
- 2 slices white bread
- 1 pearl onion, thinly sliced
- 2 cherry tomatoes, thinly sliced
- 1 ½ slices American cheese
- 1 tablespoon prepared Thousand Island salad dressing
- 2 baby dill pickles, thinly sliced

Directions:

1. Divide the beef into six equal portions and give the shape of flat discs. They should be around 1 inch in diameter.
2. Place paper towels on a microwave safe. Place the patties on the plate. Now, place another paper towel on top of the burgers.
3. Cook on high power in the microwave for about 60 – 80 seconds or until the meat is no longer pink.
4. Cut one slice of cheese into four equal squares and the half slice into two equal squares.

5. Cut 1-inch circles from the bread slices. You should have 12 circles, so use more bread slices if required.

6. To build the burgers, place six bread rounds on a serving platter. Spread the salad dressing lightly on each bread round. Place a burger on each. Place a piece of cheese, onion slice, pickle slice, and tomato slice on each. Cover each with a bread round. Fasten with toothpicks.

7. Serve.

Magic Wands

Kids will learn to dip the pretzel rods in melted chocolate and sprinkle them with colored sugar or edible sprinkles. They will also learn to line a baking sheet with wax paper.

Level: Easy

Serves: 12

Preparation time: 15 minutes

Cooking time: 5 minutes

Nutritional values per serving: 1 magic wand

Calories: 103

Fat: 4 g

Carbohydrates: 15 g

Protein: 2 g

Ingredients:

- 5 ounces pretzel rods
- ¾ cup white baking chips
- 1 – 2 tablespoons colored sugar or edible glitter
- 1 – 2 tablespoons candy stars or sprinkles

Directions:

1. Place chocolate chips in a microwave-safe bowl. Melt them in a microwave on high power for about 2 minutes or until melted completely.

2. Meanwhile, a sheet of wax paper is to be placed on a baking sheet.

3. Working with one pretzel rod at a time, dip it in melted chocolate up to half the length of the rod.

4. With your other hand, sprinkle colored sugar or edible glitter over the chocolate-dipped part and place it on the baking sheet. Set aside until the chocolate sets.

5. You can serve or place it in an airtight container to serve later.

Pigs in a Blanket

This is an easy party recipe, and kids will have fun doing it. They will learn how to wrap the little smokies with dough and line the baking sheet with parchment paper as well.

Level: Easy

Serves: 20

Preparation time: 15 minutes

Cooking time: 15 minutes

Nutritional values per serving: 1 pig in a blanket

Calories: 40

Fat: 2 g

Carbohydrates: 5 g

Protein: 1 g

Ingredients:

- 8 ounces Little Smokies
- 1 package of crescent rolls
- Poppy seeds to garnish (optional)

Directions:

1. The oven is to be preheated to 350° F.
2. Unfold the crescent. You will find pre-scored triangles on it. Cut these into triangles (along the scores) using a knife. Now, cut each triangle into three equal triangles.

3. Next, wrap one triangle over one Little smokie. This is a pig in a blanket.

4. Place it on the prepared baking sheet, with the seam side touching it. If desired, scatter poppy seeds on the blankets.

5. Repeat this with the remaining smokies and triangles and place them in the oven until they are baked until golden brown.

6. Cool for a few minutes before serving.

Birthday Cake Freezer Pops

Kids will learn to crush wafers and fill the cups with sprinkles. Older kids can be taught to use the piping bag.

Level: Easy

Serves: 9

Preparation time: 25 minutes

Cooking time: 0 minutes

Nutritional values per serving: 1 pop

Calories: 161

Fat: 7 g

Carbohydrates: 23 g

Protein: 1 g

Ingredients:

- 1/3 cup sprinkles, divided
- 1 cup 2% milk
- ½ carton (from an 8-ounce carton) of frozen whipped topping thawed
- ½ package (from a 3.4 ounces package) instant vanilla pudding mix
- 1 cup crushed vanilla wafers
- 9 disposable plastic or paper cups (3 ounces each)
- 9 wooden popsicle sticks

- 9 pieces of foil

Directions:

1. Add pudding mix and milk into a bowl and whisk until well combined. Set it aside for two minutes.

2. Place a teaspoon of sprinkles in each cup (nine cups).

3. Add whipped topping and crushed wafers When the pudding is softly set. Also, add any remaining sprinkles.

4. Spoon the mixture into a pastry or plastic bag and cut a hole at the tip of the bag of about 1-inch width.

5. Pipe the pudding mixture into the cups.

6. Cover each cup with foil. Pierce a Popsicle stick into each cup, passing through the foil.

7. Place the cups in the freezer until ready to serve.

8. Remove them from the freezer five minutes before serving. Remove them from the cups and serve.

Marshmallow Pops

These pops are easy to make and great for a kids' party. Use colored sprinkles as per the occasion (for instance, red and green for Christmas, red, white, and blue for the Fourth of July, etc.). They will learn to dip the pops and dredge them in toppings.

Level: Easy

Serves: 10

Preparation time: 30 minutes plus chilling time

Cooking time: 2 minutes

Nutritional values per serving: 1 pop, without toppings

Calories: 136

Fat: 6 g

Carbohydrates: 22 g

Protein: 1 g

Ingredients:

- 1 cup semisweet chocolate chips
- 20 large marshmallows
- 1 tablespoon canola oil
- 10 wooden popsicle sticks

For toppings:

- colored sprinkles
- toasted coconut
- toasted chopped nuts
- any other toppings of your choice

Directions:

1. Place chocolate chips and oil in a bowl and melt it in a microwave. Whisk until smooth.

2. Take a Popsicle stick and insert two marshmallows into it. Repeat this process with the remaining sticks and marshmallows.

3. Prepare a baking sheet by lining it with wax paper.

4. Dip one marshmallow-pierced stick in the melted chocolate-oil mixture. Lift it above the mixture and let the extra mixture drop.

5. Next, dredge in the chosen toppings. Finally, place on the baking sheet.

6. Chill until ready to serve.

Peach Crisp Parfait Popsicles

Kids will learn to place the ingredients in layers in the Popsicle molds.

Level: Easy

Serves: 4

Preparation time: 10 minutes plus freezing time

Cooking time: 0 minutes

Nutritional values per serving: 1 Popsicle

Calories: 167

Fat: 3 g

Carbohydrates: 28 g

Protein: 10 g

Ingredients:

- 1 carton (5.3 ounces) of fat-free vanilla Greek yogurt
- 1/8 teaspoon ground cinnamon
- ½ cup granola without raisins
- 1 teaspoon brown sugar
- 1/8 teaspoon ground nutmeg
- ½ can (from 15 ounces can) of sliced peaches in extra-light syrup or juice, drained, chopped

Directions:

1. Add yogurt, spices, and brown sugar into a bowl and stir until sugar dissolves completely.
2. Add granola and fold gently.
3. Take half the yogurt mixture and spoon equal quantities into 4 Popsicle molds.
4. Take half the chopped peach and divide them into four portions. Place one portion over the yogurt layer in each Popsicle.
5. Repeat the steps 3 and 4 to make two more layers.
6. Insert Popsicle sticks and place in the freezer until ready to serve.

Pizza Pasta Skewers

Kids will learn to thread the skewers with pasta and garnish it with your instructions. They will also learn to divide the pasta equally into six portions and line the baking sheet with parchment paper.

Level: Easy

Serves: 6

Preparation time: 15 minutes

Cooking time: 20 minutes

Nutritional values per serving: 1 skewer

Calories: 168

Fat: 8 g

Carbohydrates: 17 g

Protein: 8 g

Ingredients:

- 4 ounces penne pasta
- 1 cup shredded mozzarella cheese
- 1 ounce mini pepperoni
- chili flakes to taste (optional)

- 6 tablespoon marinara sauce
- 1.5 ounces Kalamata olives
- ¼ cup corn kernels

Directions:

1. Check the cooking instructions on the package of pasta and cook the pasta until al dente. The pasta needs to cool completely before threading onto the skewers.
2. Set the oven temperature to 450° F and allow it to preheat.
3. Divide the pasta equally into six portions. Each portion should have 10 to 12 pasta.
4. Take six skewers and thread one portion of pasta onto each skewer. Brush one tablespoon of marinara sauce on each skewer and lay it on the baking sheet.
5. Now sprinkle cheese over the skewers. Scatter corn and olives over the skewers. Place pepperoni slices.
6. Place the baking sheet in the oven and bake until cheese melts. Garnish with chili flakes and serve.

Ricotta, Blueberry, and Grape Toasts

Kids will learn to spread the butter and ricotta and place the fruit mixture on top.

Level: Easy

Serves: 2

Preparation time: 10 minutes

Cooking time: 0 minutes

Nutritional values per serving: 1 toast

Calories: 299

Fat: 14 g

Carbohydrates: 36 g

Protein: 9 g

Ingredients:

- 1/8 cup toasted, sliced almonds
- ¼ cup blueberries
- 1/3 cup red seedless grapes, halved
- ½ tablespoon fresh lemon juice
- ½ teaspoon grated lemon zest
- 2 pieces halved baguette (6 inches each)
- ¼ cup ricotta cheese
- 1 tablespoon unsalted butter, softened
- salt to taste
- freshly ground pepper to taste

Directions:

1. Preheat the oven to 350° F.
2. Combine honey and lemon juice in a bowl. Add blueberries and grapes and stir.
3. Combine ricotta and lemon zest in another bowl.

4. Spread ½ tablespoon butter on the cut part of each baguette half and place on a baking sheet. Toast the baguette in the oven until light brown and crispy.

5. Season the toasts with salt and pepper. Spread two tablespoons of the ricotta mixture on each baguette half.

6. Place each on a plate. Divide the fruit mixture equally and spread it over the toast. Drizzle any liquid from the bowl over the baguette. Garnish with almond slices and serve with honey, if desired.

Fun Cooking Activities

Breakfast Charcuterie Board

You make the waffles and let the kids arrange the charcuterie board creatively. Don't forget to teach them to rinse the fruits before placing it on the board.

Level: Easy

Serves: a small family of 2-3 persons

Preparation time: 20 minutes

Cooking time: 15 minutes

Nutritional values per serving: 1 board

Calories: 385.5

Fat: 15.5 g

Carbohydrates: 56.5 g

Protein: 8 g

Ingredients:

For mini waffles:

- 1 ¼ cups buttermilk pancake mix
- 1 ½ tablespoon salted butter, melted, cooled
- ½ teaspoon vanilla extract
- ¾ cup cold half-and-half
- 1 large egg white

For the spreads:

- 3 tablespoons raspberry jam
- 4 tablespoons maple syrup
- 3 tablespoons hazelnut spread

For the fruit:

- 2 mandarin oranges, peeled
- ½ pound strawberries

- 4 ounces blueberries
- 4 ounces raspberries
- ½ large ruby grapefruit, sliced
- ¾ cup green grapes

Directions:

1. Plug in your mini waffle iron and let it preheat.
2. Whisk pancake mix, butter, half and half, and vanilla in a bowl until well incorporated, making sure not to overmix. If you find a few small lumps, that is okay.
3. Whisk egg white in another bowl until there is much foam.
4. Add the egg white into the bowl of pancake batter and fold gently.
5. Spoon batter into the preheated waffle iron and close the lid. Let the waffle cook for 2 – 3 minutes or until golden brown.
6. Remove the waffle and place it on the charcuterie board. You can use a tray as the board.
7. Repeat making the waffles until all the batter is gone. You should have 8 – 10 mini waffles.

8. To arrange the ingredients on the board, Measure the spreads using three different spoons and place them in different bowls. Leave the spoon in each bowl. Place the bowls on the board.

9. Place the waffles in a spiral or any other creative manner. Lay the grapefruit slices on any corner of the board. Arrange the berries in any manner you please. You can keep one particular fruit at each corner if you don't have any specific ideas. Preferably cover the whole board with the ingredients.

10. Serve.

Reindeer Bites

Let the kids decorate the face of the reindeer by breaking the pretzels in half. Older kids can be taught to form balls from the mixture. Moisten their hands with water to prevent sticking. Teach them to line the serving platter with parchment paper.

Level: Easy

Serves: 8

Preparation time: 15 minutes

Cooking time: 0 minutes

Nutritional values per serving: 1 bite

Calories: 123

Fat: 5 g

Carbohydrates: 18 g

Protein: 3 g

Ingredients:

- 1 ¼ cups + 1/8 cup old-fashioned oats
- ¼ cup honey
- 8 red chocolate candy pieces
- ¼ cup smooth peanut butter
- 8 small pretzels, broken into two halves

- 16 candy eyes

Directions:

1. Finely grind the oats in a blender.

2. Add peanut butter and honey into a bowl and stir well. Stir in the ground oats.

3. Using a mini ice cream scooper (2 tablespoons), scoop the mixture and place on a plate. Roll the mixture between your palms and shape it into a ball. Place on the prepared serving platter.

4. Repeat the previous step and make the remaining balls. Place them on the plate, leaving sufficient space between them.

5. Now, insert each half of the pretzel to create antlers of the reindeer. Place two candy eyes to make the eyes and make the nose using one red chocolate candy piece.

Party Charcuterie Board

Let the kids arrange the ingredients on the Charcuterie board themselves. This is a great outlet for their creativity.

Level: Easy

Serves: 10

Preparation time: 15 minutes

Cooking time: 15 minutes

Nutritional values per serving: 8 ounces mixture of different ingredients

Calories: 508

Fat: 29 g

Carbohydrates: 43 g

Protein: 20 g

Ingredients:

For the fruits:

- ½ cup raspberries
- ½ cup strawberries
- ½ cup blueberries
- ½ cup grapes
- 1 apple, cored, thinly sliced

For the meat:

- 4 ounces pepperoni slices
- 4 ounces of genoa salami
- 4 ounces ham
- 10 mini hot dogs

Other ingredients:

- ½ cup cheddar cheese cubes
- 4 ounces mozzarella slices
- ½ cup pickles

- ½ cup pitted olives
- 6 ounces goldfish crackers
- 4 ounces pretzels
- 4 ounces crackers
- 10 toasted bread slices

Directions:

1. Take a large tray. You can use serving bowls to store some of the ingredients. They can be placed in the corners. This is just a suggestion.

2. You can place the ingredients in whatever manner you please. Make sure to use the board fully.

Monster Mash Potato

This is a fun activity, especially for Halloween. Teach your kids to mash the potatoes and make monster faces using the mash. Suggestions to make the monster (eyes, nose, etc.) are listed under the ingredients. Older kids can be taught to pipe the mashed potatoes.

Level: Easy

Serves: 8

Preparation time: 20 minutes

Cooking time: 20 minutes

Nutritional values per serving: 1 monster face base of mashed potato, without the decoration.

Calories: 257

Fat: 7 g

Carbohydrates: 44 g

Protein: 6 g

Ingredients:

- 4 pounds baked potatoes
- 2 cups milk

- salt to taste

- ground pepper to taste

- 6 cloves garlic, peeled, grated (optional)

- 4 tablespoons butter

For the decorations:

- broccoli florets, shredded cheese, or boiled spaghetti for hair

- bell pepper strips or strips of chives for lips

- green peas or olives for the eyes

- anything else of your choice

Directions:

1. Peel and quarter the potatoes. Boil a pot of water over high heat with about 1 ½ teaspoons of salt added to it.

2. Drop the potato chunks and garlic into the pot. Turn the heat to medium and cook for about 15 – 20 minutes.

3. When the potatoes are nearly done cooking, warm the butter and milk in a small saucepan over low heat. When the butter melts, turn off the heat.

4. Remove the pot of potatoes from the heat. Drain the water from the potatoes and transfer them to a bowl.

5. Pour the milk mixture into the bowl. Mash the potatoes with a potato masher until well combined and very smooth.

6. Divide the mashed potatoes into eight equal portions and place each on a plate. You can use a large cookie cutter or egg ring and place the mash inside to form the face. You can also place a portion of mashed potato in a piping bag and pipe it into a face on the plate.

7. Now, shape the mashed potatoes into the shape of a face (round, oval, etc.). Decorate with eyes, nose, horns, lips, ears, etc. You can use almond slivers to make teeth.

Pancake Time

Kids will learn to pour and mix the batter. You can teach them to use cookie cutters to pour the batter into different shapes. Make sure they do it under adult supervision. They can also make fun shapes using round pancakes like a teddy bear (small round pancakes for the ears and a bigger round pancake for the face). They can make eyes, nose, and mouth using berries or fruit.

Level: Easy

Serves: 8

Preparation time: 15 minutes

Cooking time: 20-30 minutes

Nutritional values per serving: 1 pancake, without toppings

Calories: 350

Fat: 10 g

Carbohydrates: 55 g

Protein: 10 g

Ingredients:

- 4 cups all-purpose flour
- 1 teaspoon baking soda

- 3 teaspoons baking powder
- ½ teaspoon salt
- 4 cups buttermilk
- 2 teaspoons vanilla extract
- 6 tablespoons sugar
- 4 large eggs
- ½ cup melted unsalted butter
- 2 teaspoons ground cinnamon
- maple syrup or any other syrup to serve or decorate
- toppings to decorate, like strawberry slices, blueberries, banana slices, etc.
- Peanut butter or any other nut butter

Directions:

1. Sift the flour, baking powder, salt, baking soda, and cinnamon into a large bowl. Stir in the sugar.

2. Crack eggs into another bowl. Add buttermilk, vanilla extract, and melted butter and whisk until well combined.

3. Pour the egg mixture into the bowl with the flour mixture and stir until just incorporated.

4. Place a non-stick pan over medium heat. If you want to teach your kid to pour the batter into the pan, make sure the batter is in a cup with a spout. They will not be able to handle a ladle.

5. Scoop out ¼ cup of batter and pour into the pan. Soon bubbles will form on top of the pancake. Show the kids this formation of bubbles. Lift a bit of the bottom side of the pancake with a spatula. If it is golden brown, turn the sides and cook the other side. If not, wait a few more seconds until it turns golden brown.

6. After making a few pancakes, you can add some cocoa powder to the batter to make chocolate pancakes. You can substitute flour with whole-wheat flour or use pancake pre-mix to make the pancakes.

7. Now decorate the pancakes and serve. Strawberry or banana slices can be used as eyes or nose. Blueberries can be used as the pupil of the eyes. You can arrange many blueberries to

look like the mouth. Before decorating, you can spread some peanut butter. The ideas are endless.

Eggs in a Nest (Spaghetti and Meatball Muffin Bites)

Kids will learn to make the nests using spaghetti. Let them be creative and they will learn portion control as well. Let them grease the muffin pan as well.

Level: Easy

Serves: 6

Preparation time: 15 minutes plus 15 minutes chilling time

Cooking time: 45 minutes

Nutritional values per serving: 1 egg in a nest

Calories: 198

Fat: 9 g

Carbohydrates: 17 g

Protein: 11 g

Ingredients:

- 3 ounces of uncooked spaghetti
- ¾ cup grated parmesan cheese, divided
- 6 cooked meatballs (1 ounce each)
- 2 teaspoons olive oil
- ¾ cup tomato-based pasta sauce

Directions:

1. Boil a pot of water with a little salt. Add spaghetti and cook until al dente. Drain off the water and place it in a bowl. Drizzle olive oil and toss well.
2. Place it in the refrigerator for 15 minutes.
3. Meanwhile, preheat the oven to 375° F. Grease a 6-count muffin pan by brushing with oil or using cooking oil spray.
4. Add ½ cup of parmesan cheese to the bowl of spaghetti and toss well. Using easy-grip tongs, lift some of the spaghetti

and place it in a muffin cup, twirling it as you place it, making a nest. Make sure all the cups have almost equal spaghetti. This way, they learn portion control.

5. Spoon a tablespoon of pasta sauce into each cup over the spaghetti.

6. Place a meatball in each cup. Spoon a tablespoon of pasta sauce over each meatball. Sprinkle the remaining parmesan cheese on top of the meatballs.

7. Bake for about 20-25 minutes. When done, carefully remove the nests from the muffin cups and serve. You may have to loosen the edges of the nests with a knife.

8. You can serve it as is or have the kids decorate the tops of the nests with herbs and vegetable strips.

Frosted Sugar Cookies

Kids will learn to roll the dough and cut the cookies using different cookie cutters. Let them use their imagination and frost and garnish the cookies. Baking and cooling the cookies will also teach them to be patient.

Level: Medium

Serves: 36 cookies

Preparation time: 20 minutes plus chilling time

Cooking time: 6-8 minutes per batch

Nutritional values per serving: 1 frosted cookie

Calories: 117

Fat: 5 g

Carbohydrates: 17 g

Protein: 1 g

Ingredients:

- ¾ cup unsalted butter, softened
- 2 eggs
- 2 ½ cups all-purpose flour plus more for dusting

- ½ teaspoon salt
- 1 cup granulated sugar
- ¾ teaspoon vanilla extract or almond/coconut/peppermint extract
- 1 teaspoon baking powder

For the frosting:

- 1 cup powdered sugar
- ½ tablespoon light corn syrup or honey
- edible food colouring of choice (optional)
- 1-2 tablespoons milk
- ½ teaspoon vanilla extract or almond/coconut/peppermint extract

Directions:

1. You can knead the dough using your hands or with a stand mixer.

2. This recipe uses a stand mixer. Fix the bowl of the stand mixer with the paddle attachment.

3. Add butter and sugar and beat until creamy. Add the eggs and the chosen extract and mix until well incorporated.

4. Combine flour, salt, and baking powder in another bowl. Mix the flour mixture with the butter mixture in batches. Mix until dough is formed.

5. Make 2- 3 portions of the dough and flatten them. Wrap the discs in individual plastic wraps and place them in the refrigerator for 2- 4 hours. If you are short of time, you may freeze the dough for about 20 minutes.

6. Preheat the oven to 400° F.

7. Dust a part of your countertop with flour. Take one disc of dough from the refrigerator and place it on the floured area. Using a rolling pin, roll the dough until it is about 1/8-1/4 inch thick.

8. Cut the cookies using cookie cutters and place them on a baking sheet (do not grease the baking sheet). Use two or more baking sheets.

9. Repeat the process with the remaining discs (step 7&8).

10. You can collect the scrap dough remaining after cutting the cookies, re-roll the dough, and cut more cookies.

11. Place a baking sheet in the oven and bake for 6 to 8 minutes or until the underside is light golden brown.

12. With a metal spatula, take the cookies from the baking sheet and place them on a wire rack. Let them cool completely.

13. Bake the cookies in batches.

14. While the cookies are cooling, prepare the sugar cookie frosting: Place powdered sugar, corn syrup, and vanilla extract in a bowl. Preferably use corn syrup. By doing this, the frosting is comparatively drier than honey. Honey makes it sticky and unsuitable while storing the cookies in a pile. Add a tablespoon of milk and stir until well combined. You need thick frosting for piping or spreading the frosting. If you want to dip the cookies, make the frosting thinner. For kids to frost, thicker frosting is recommended.

15. So add more milk according to the preferred consistency. Add the preferred food coloring.

16. When the cookies are fully cooled, frost them. If desired, decorate with sprinkles, but make sure to do it before the frosting sets.

Thumbprint Cookies

The kids will have fun making their thumbprints on each cookie. They should place a little jam in the dent made by their thumbprint. They can use 2–3 different jams on the cookies. Older kids can be taught to make balls of dough.

Level: Medium

Serves: 40

Preparation time: 25 minutes

Cooking time: 15 minutes per batch

Nutritional values per serving: 1 thumbprint cookie with jam and frosting

Calories: 139

Fat: 5 g

Carbohydrates: 23 g

Protein: 1 g

Ingredients:

For the cookies:

- 2/3 cup powdered sugar
- 2/3 cup white sugar or as required
- ½ teaspoon fine salt
- 2 ½ cups all-purpose flour
- 2 large egg yolks
- 1 cup unsalted butter at room temperature
- 2 teaspoons vanilla extract
- ¼ teaspoon almond extract
- 1 cup fruit jam, divided

For the icing:

- 2 tablespoons milk or more if required
- 2 cups powdered sugar or more if required

Directions:

1. Preheat the oven to 325° F. Prepare a baking sheet by lining it with a silicone mat or parchment paper.
2. Fix the bowl of the stand mixer with the paddle attachment or use an electric hand mixer and a mixing bowl.
3. Add butter and powdered sugar and beat until creamy. Add the egg yolks, salt, vanilla, and almond extract and mix until well incorporated.
4. Add flour and mix until just incorporated.
5. Place white sugar on a plate.
6. Take out 1 tablespoon of the dough and shape it into a ball using your hands. Next, dredge the ball in white sugar. Roll the ball once again using your palms and place it on the baking sheet.

7. Repeat this process. Make sure to leave sufficient space between the cookies. Now press the balls slightly with your fingers.

8. If you like roundish cookies, make a dent in the centre of the cookie with the tip of your finger, and you can fill less jam.

9. If you want more jam in the cookies, flatten the cookies. Make a dent in the cookies using your thumb and fill will jam. You can fill some cookies with one flavor of jam, some with another.

10. Tap lightly on the countertop Once a baking sheet is filled. You can place it in the oven while you prepare the other cookies. Bake for 12 – 15 minutes or until they turn light golden in color.

11. Bake the cookies in batches. Let the cookies come to room temperature.

12. While the cookies are cooling, make the icing: Place powdered sugar in a bowl. Add two tablespoons of milk and

stir until smooth. Add more milk if required and spoon the icing into a piping bag with a small, round tip.

13. Pipe the icing over the cookies in whatever manner you please and let it rest for 15 minutes. Let the icing set before storing.

14. You can also store the baked cookies in an airtight container and ice them before serving.

Owl Toast

As the name suggests, let the kids decorate the toast to resemble an owl. Give them all the ingredients and let them get to work.

Level: Easy

Serves: 2

Preparation time: 5 minutes

Cooking time: 2 minutes

Nutritional values per serving: 1 toast

Calories: 274

Fat: 4.5 g

Carbohydrates: 55.2 g

Protein: 7.4 g

Ingredients:

- 2 English muffins, split
- 8 blueberries
- 4 strawberries
- 2 small bananas
- 2 tablespoons peanut butter

Directions:

1. Pop the English muffin halves in a toaster and toast the muffins to the desired crunchiness.

2. Spread ½ tablespoon peanut butter on one side of each muffin half (on the cut side).

3. Peel and cut the bananas into thick, round slices. These can be used to make the eyes.

4. The blueberries can be used to make the pupils.

5. Cut the strawberry into slices lengthwise and use these slices to make a beak and wings.

6. Decorate the toasts like an owl and serve.

Banana Muffins

Kids will learn to measure the ingredients and stir the batter. They will also learn about patience as they wait for the muffins to bake and cool. Teach them to mash the bananas and grease the muffin cups and place disposable liners in it.

Level: Easy

Serves: 24

Preparation time: 15 minutes

Cooking time: 25 minutes

Nutritional values per serving: 1 muffin

Calories: 186

Fat: 6 g

Carbohydrates: 32 g

Protein: 3 g

Ingredients:

- 3 cups all-purpose flour
- 2 teaspoons baking soda
- 2 teaspoons baking powder
- 1 teaspoon salt
- 1 ½ cups white sugar
- 2/3 cup butter, melted
- 2 large eggs
- 6 large bananas

Directions:

1. Preheat the oven to 350° F. Prepare two muffin pans of 12 counts each (or use only one pan and bake them in 2 batches) by greasing them with cooking oil. Place a disposable liner in each cup.

2. Sift the flour into a large bowl with salt, baking soda and baking powder.

3. Peel the bananas and break them into pieces. Place the banana pieces in a large bowl and mash with a fork.

4. Mix eggs, sugar, and melted butter until well combined.

5. Add the flour mixture and mix until well combined.

6. Fill the muffin cups with batter up to 2/3 the height of the cup.

7. Place the muffin pan in the oven and bake for 25-30 minutes or until a toothpick pierced in the center of the muffin looks clean when pulled out without any batter stuck on it (a few crumbs are okay, but not batter sticking).

8. Let the muffins cool on the countertop for about 10 minutes. Remove them from the pan and place them on a wire rack to cool.

9. Serve. You can save the leftovers in an airtight container in the refrigerator or freeze them in re-sealable bags.

Sleeping Bag Blondies

Let the kids learn to make the sleeping bag, decorate the face, make hair, etc. The older kids can learn how to pipe the frosting and baking the blondies too.

Level: Medium

Serves: 8

Preparation time: 20 minutes

Cooking time: 30-35 minutes

Nutritional values per serving: 1 sleeping bag blondie

Calories: 392

Fat: 16 g

Carbohydrates: 59 g

Protein: 3 g

Ingredients:

For the brownie:

- ½ cup butter, softened
- ½ cup packed brown sugar
- ½ cup sugar
- 1 cup chopped pecans (optional)
- 1 teaspoon vanilla extract
- 1 large egg at room temperature
- 1 cup self-rising flour

For the decoration:

- ¾ cup white frosting
- 4 large marshmallows
- edible pen
- assorted sprinkles

- 2-4 assorted gel food coloring
- 8 miniature, round vanilla wafers

Directions:

1. Preheat the oven to 325° F. Prepare a small, rectangular baking pan by lining it with a large foil so that the bottom and sides of the baking pan are covered.

2. Brush the foil with oil or spray some cooking spray.

3. Place butter, brown sugar, and sugar in a mixing bowl. Beat with an electric hand mixer until creamy and light.

4. Add egg and vanilla and beat until well combined.

5. Add flour and beat until the batter is smooth. Fold in the pecans if using.

6. Spoon the batter into the baking pan and place in the oven for about 30-35 minutes. Check if the brownie is ready by inserting a toothpick in the center of the brownie. Remove it and check if any batter is stuck on it. If it is stuck, you must

bake for a few more minutes. If there isn't any batter stuck, the brownie is ready.

7. Place the brownie on a wire rack.

8. Now, lift the brownie with the help of the foil and place it on your cutting board.

9. Trim all the edges a little (about ½ inch). Cut the brownie into two halves lengthwise. Cut each half into four equal bars crosswise. These are the sleeping bags.

10. Distribute the frosting into 2-4 bowls. Add the desired colour to the bowls. You can leave one bowl as it is and use it as white.

11. Spoon the frosting into small, 2-4 different piping bags, making sure to retain a little of each frosting that will be used later to fix the wafers.

12. Snip off the ends of the piping bag and pipe it over the brownie bars. You can keep the frosting smooth or run the back of a spoon to make any design.

13. Cut each marshmallow into two halves and use it as a pillow. Keep it with the cut side down on one end of the bar.

14. You can make faces on the wafers with an edible marker or pipe the frosting, giving the shape of mouth, eyes, etc.

15. Using some retained frosting, place a bit on the marshmallow and stick a wafer on it.

16. Pipe some frosting on the face to make hair. Garnish with sprinkles if desired.

Bonus Recipes

Healthy Oatmeal Muffins

In this recipe, you can teach them to measure the ingredients and mix the batter. Teach them to line up the muffin pan with disposable liners. Older children can be taught to operate on the blender.

Serves: 6

Preparation time: 5 minutes

Cooking time: 20 minutes

Nutritional values per serving: 1 muffin

Calories: 102

Fat: 2 g

Carbohydrates: 17 g

Protein: 44 g

Ingredients:

- 1 cup rolled oats
- ¼ teaspoon baking soda
- ¾ teaspoon baking powder
- 1/8 teaspoon salt
- ½ cup vanilla Greek or plain yoghurt
- 1 ½ tablespoons honey or maple syrup
- ½ cup blueberries (optional)
- 1 large egg
- ½ teaspoon vanilla extract
- 1 large banana

Directions:

1. Set the oven temperature to 350°F and allow it to preheat.
2. Place a disposable cupcake liner in each cup of a six-count muffin pan.
3. Peel and break the banana into smaller pieces, or let the child cut the banana with a blunt knife.

4. Place rolled oats, baking soda, baking powder, salt, yoghurt, maple syrup, egg, vanilla extract and banana in a blender. Blend the contents until they are free from lumps.
5. Spoon equal quantities of the batter into the muffin cups.
6. Place the muffin pan in the oven and bake for about 20 minutes. Keep a watch over the muffins at around 17-18 minutes through baking.
7. To check if the muffins are done, insert a toothpick in the centre of the muffin and take it out. If the muffin has no batter stuck onto it, it is ready.
8. Cool the muffins in the pan for 10-12 minutes. Remove them from the cups and place them on a wire rack to cool. Once cooled, put them in an airtight container. They can be stored in the refrigerator for about 15 days.

Fruit and Granola Yogurt Bowl

Let kids create their yoghurt bowl with the ingredients. They will be happy to choose their toppings.

Serves: 2

Preparation time: 10 minutes

Cooking time: 0 minutes

Total time: 10 minutes

Nutritional value per serving:

1 bowl, without optional toppings

Calories: 352

Fat: 7 g

Carbohydrates: 54 g

Protein: 22 g

Ingredients:

- 12 ounces plain or flavoured Greek yoghurt, unsweetened
- 2 cups fresh fruit
- ½ cup granola
- 4 teaspoons honey or maple syrup

Choose fruits:

- blueberries or strawberries, blackberries or mixed berries
- mango
- banana
- kiwi
- pineapple
- peach

Toppings: Optional

- peanut butter, almond butter, sunflower butter etc.
- seeds or nuts of your choice or use a combination
- ground cinnamon
- hemp hearts
- chia seeds
- shredded coconut
- Mini chocolate chips

Directions:

1. Divide yoghurt into two bowls. You can choose one particular fruit or use a mixture of fruits.

2. Top with ¼ cup granola and 1 cup fruit in each bowl. Trickle two teaspoons of honey in each bowl. You can add any other optional toppings if desired.
3. Serve.

Bacon Cream Cheese Pinwheels

Teach the kids how to mix the spread ingredients. Then, roll the dough and spread the mixture over it. Older kids can learn to roll the dough and cut it into pinwheels.

Serves: 12

Preparation time: 15 minutes

Cooking time: 15 minutes

Nutritional values per serving: 1 pinwheel

Calories: 58

Fat: 4 g

Carbohydrates: 4 g

Protein: 1 g

Ingredients:

- 1.5 ounces cream cheese, softened
- ½ teaspoon milk
- 2 ½ strips of bacon, cooked, finely chopped
- 1 tablespoon finely chopped onion
- 4 ounces refrigerated crescent rolls

Directions:

1. Preheat the oven to 375°F.
2. Add cream cheese and milk into a bowl and stir until well combined. Add onion and stir.
3. Dust the countertop with some flour. Unfold the dough and roll the dough with a rolling pin. Press on the dotted lines so that the dots are sealed.
4. Smear the cream cheese mixture over the rolled dough.
5. Scatter bacon over the cream cheese layer. Start with the longer side and roll the dough to the opposite side. Press the edges to seal.

6. Cut the roll into 12 equal pieces. Place the pinwheels on a baking sheet (do not grease the baking sheet) with the cut side visible on top.
7. Pop the baking sheet into the oven until golden brown.

Chocolate Chia Pudding

Let the kids measure the ingredients and place them in the blender. Older kids can learn how to operate the blender under your guidance. They can also cut the banana with a blunt knife or break it into pieces.

Serves: 1

Preparation time: 5 minutes

Cooking time: 0 minutes plus chilling time

Nutritional values per serving: 1 jar

Calories: 271

Fat: 1 g

Carbohydrates: 38 g

Protein: 10 g

Ingredients:

- ½ cup milk of your choice
- ½ tablespoon maple syrup
- ½ tablespoon cocoa powder
- ½ teaspoon vanilla extract
- ½ tablespoon peanut butter
- ½ banana
- ½ teaspoon ground cinnamon
- 1 ½ tablespoons chia seeds

Directions:

1. Place banana and chia seeds in a blender. Next, place the peanut butter, cocoa powder, cinnamon, vanilla extract, and maple syrup.
2. Finally, pour the milk over the ingredients and blitz until free from lumps.

3. Pour into a Mason jar and keep it covered in the refrigerator for 5-8 hours.
4. Serve chilled.

Chickpea & Quinoa Grain Bowls

Let the children learn to build the grain bowl.

Serves: 2

Preparation time: 15 minutes

Cooking time: 20 minutes

Nutritional values per serving: 1 bowl

Calories: 503

Fat: 17 g

Carbohydrates: 75 g

Protein: 18 g

Ingredients:

- 2 cups cooked quinoa
- 1 cup cucumber slices
- ½ avocado, peeled, pitted, diced
- 2/3 cup cooked or canned chickpeas, rinsed, drained
- 1 cup cherry tomatoes, halved
- 1/8 cup finely chopped roasted red pepper
- 2 tablespoons water plus extra if required
- salt to taste
- 6 tablespoons hummus
- 2 tablespoons fresh lemon juice
- 2 teaspoons chopped fresh parsley (optional)
- pepper to taste

Directions:

1. Divide equally the quinoa and chickpeas among two wide bowls.
2. Scatter tomatoes, cucumber, and avocado on top.
3. Combine roasted red pepper, seasonings, parsley, water, hummus, and lemon juice in a bowl.
4. Drizzle the dressing over the bowl and serve.

Sweet Potato & Bean Quesadillas

Teach the kids to scrub a sweet potato. They can prick the sweet potato as well.

Serves: 2

Preparation time: 5 minutes

Cooking time: 8 minutes

Nutritional values per serving: 1 quesadilla and three tablespoons of salsa

Calories: 306

Fat: 8 g

Carbohydrates: 46 g

Protein: 11 g

Ingredients:

- 1 medium sweet potato, scrubbed
- 1/3 cup canned or cooked black beans, drained, rinsed
- 6 tablespoons salsa
- 2 whole-wheat tortillas (8 inches each)
- ¼ cup shredded pepper Jack cheese

Directions:

1. Prick the sweet potato at different places using a fork.
2. Place it in a microwave-safe bowl. Cook on high in a microwave for 7 – 8 minutes or until soft.
3. When the sweet potato cools slightly, cut it into two halves. Mash each half and spread on one half of each tortilla, leaving about ½ inch around the edges.
4. Scatter half the beans and cheese over the sweet potato on each tortilla.
5. Lift the other half of the tortilla and place it over the filling. The edges of the tortilla should meet. Press to adhere.
6. Heat a pan over medium heat. When hot, add the quesadillas and cook until the underside is crisp and brown.
7. Turn the quesadilla over and cook the other side as well.

8. Instead of cooking in a pan, you can bake the quesadillas in an oven until crisp.
9. Cut into wedges and serve along with salsa.

Avocado, Tomato & Chicken Sandwich

The kids can learn how to scoop the avocado and mash as well. They can make the sandwich, too. Older kids can be taught to use a toaster to toast the bread slices.

Serves: 2

Preparation time: 5 minutes

Cooking time: 0 minutes

Nutritional values per serving: 1 sandwich

Calories: 347

Fat: 12 g

Carbohydrates: 28 g

Protein: 31 g

Ingredients:

- 4 slices multigrain bread
- 6 ounces cooked, sliced, skinless, boneless chicken breast
- ½ ripe avocado
- 4 tomato slices

Directions:

1. Pop the bread slices into a toaster and toast to the desired crunchiness.
2. Scoop the avocado into a bowl and mash using a fork.
3. Take half the avocado and spread it on a slice of toasted bread. Repeat this step with another slice of bread and the remaining avocado.
4. Place an equal number of chicken slices over these two toasts.
5. Cover with the remaining slices of toast to complete the sandwich. Cut into the desired shape and serve.

Roast Chicken & Sweet Potato

Teach the kids to flavour the chicken. Let them smear the mixture over the chicken. They may not like messy hands, but they need to learn.

Serves: 2

Preparation time: 15 minutes

Cooking time: 15 minutes

Nutritional values per serving: 1 plate

Calories: 408

Fat: 17 g

Carbohydrates: 34 g

Protein: 27 g

Ingredients:

- 1 tablespoon whole-grain mustard or Dijon mustard
- 1 tablespoon extra-virgin olive oil, divided
- ¼ freshly ground black pepper
- 1 medium sweet potato, peeled, cut into 1-inch cubes
- 1 tablespoon chopped fresh thyme or one teaspoon dried thyme
- ¼ teaspoon salt, divided
- 1 pound bone-in chicken thighs, skinless
- ½ sizeable red onion, cut into 1-inch wedges

Directions:

1. Place the rack in the lower third position in the oven. Place a baking sheet in the oven.
2. Preheat the oven to 450° F along with the baking sheet.
3. Add mustard, ½ tablespoon of oil, thyme, 1/8 teaspoon pepper, and 1/8 teaspoon salt into a bowl and mix. Smear this mixture over the chicken.
4. Combine sweet potatoes, onion, 1/8 teaspoon pepper, 1/8 teaspoon salt, and ½ tablespoon of oil.
5. Take out the baking sheet. Place the vegetables on the baking sheet and the chicken over the vegetables.

6. Place the baking sheet in the oven and roast until the vegetables are tender and the chicken is cooked. The internal temperature of the chicken in the thickest part should show 165° F on the meat thermometer.
7. Distribute the vegetables equally onto two plates. Place equal quantities of chicken over the vegetables and serve.

Steak Bites & Mushrooms

Teach the kids to pat dry the steak cubes. Let them drizzle the oil over the steak cubes.

Serves: 1

Preparation time: 5 minutes

Cooking time: 10 minutes

Nutritional values per serving: Without melted butter

Calories: 401

Fat: 29 g

Carbohydrates: 3 g

Protein: 32 g

Ingredients:

- 5.3 ounces steak, cut into ½ inch cubes, rinsed
- 2 teaspoons butter or olive oil
- ¼ teaspoon garlic powder or to taste
- freshly cracked black pepper to taste
- melted butter to serve (optional)
- finely chopped parsley to garnish
- chilli flakes to garnish
- 1/3 cup halved mushrooms
- 1/3 teaspoon Worcestershire sauce
- flaky salt to taste

Directions:

1. Pat the steak pieces dry with paper towels. Add the steak and mushrooms to a bowl.

2. Pour olive oil or melt two teaspoons of butter and pour over the steak pieces. Mix well with garlic powder, pepper, salt, and Worcestershire sauce.
3. Place the steak in a pan and spread it all over the pan. Do not stir for about a minute. Now flip them over and cook for a minute. Remove the steak and place in a bowl.
4. Add mushrooms to the pan and cook for a few minutes until the mushrooms are tender.
5. Transfer mushrooms into the bowl with steak bites. Sprinkle parsley on top. Drizzle melted butter, if using, and toss well. Sprinkle salt and pepper, if desired. Toss well.
6. Serve.

Sweet Potato Smoothie Bowl

Let the kids learn to slice and freeze bananas. Let them know to measure and place the ingredients in a blender. Older kids can learn to press the buttons on the blender. Let them put the toppings on the smoothie. They can choose their toppings if they do not like the suggested toppings.

Serves: 1

Preparation time: 10 minutes

Cooking time: 0 minutes

Nutritional values per serving: 1 smoothie bowl with toppings given in the recipe

Calories: 400

Fat: 5 g

Carbohydrates: 87 g

Protein: 9 g

Ingredients:

- 1 medium sweet potato, roasted, cubed
- ¼ cup rolled oats
- ½ teaspoon vanilla extract
- 1 medium banana, sliced
- 2 tablespoons unsweetened soymilk

- ¼ teaspoon ground cinnamon
- ½ tablespoon chia seeds
- 3-4 tablespoons water

For the toppings:

- ¼ mango, peeled, diced
- ¼ cup fresh raspberries
- chopped fresh mint leaves
- ½ kiwi, peeled, thinly sliced

Directions:

1. Place the banana slices on a tray and freeze for 2 hours or until they are hard.
2. Place sweet potato, oats, vanilla, chia seeds, banana slices, and cinnamon in the blender. Pour soymilk and water and blend until there are no lumps. It can take a little longer to blend (a couple of minutes or longer). Add some water or soymilk if required.

3. Pour the smoothie into a bowl. Scatter mango, raspberries, kiwi slices, and mint leaves on top and serve.

Turkey Apple Cheddar Sandwich

You can involve the kids at the party to assemble the sandwiches.

Serves: 2

Preparation time: 6-7 minutes

Cooking time: 0 minutes

Nutritional values per serving: 1 sandwich

Calories: 440

Fat: 23 g

Carbohydrates: 31 g

Protein: 23 g

Ingredients:

- 4 slices whole-wheat sandwich bread

- 4 ounces low or reduced-sodium deli turkey
- 10-12 thin apple slices
- 2 tablespoons mayonnaise
- 2 ounces sliced cheddar cheese

Directions:

1. ½ tablespoon of mayonnaise will be spread on one side of each bread slice.
2. Place equal quantities of turkey, apple, and cheese slices on two bread slices.
3. Cover with the remaining two bread slices with the mayonnaise side facing down.
4. Cut into triangles and serve.

Black Bean and Sweet Potato Salad

Teach the kiddos to whisk the dressing. Let them season the sweet potato with spices and oil. Let them learn to toss the ingredients together.

Serves: 2

Preparation time: 15 minutes

Cooking time: 25 minutes

Nutritional values per serving: 1 plate

Calories: 291

Fat: 11 g

Carbohydrates: 42 g

Protein: 8 g

Ingredients:

- ½ pound sweet potatoes, peeled, cut into ¾ into cubes
- ¼ teaspoon ground cumin
- coarse salt to taste
- black pepper to taste
- ½ can (from 14.5 ounces can) black beans, rinsed, drained
- ¼ cup chopped fresh cilantro
- 1 ½ tablespoons olive oil, divided
- 1/8 teaspoon red pepper flakes (optional)

- 1 tablespoon fresh lime juice
- ¼ red onion, finely chopped

Directions:

1. Set the oven temperature to 50°F and allow it to preheat.
2. Place the sweet potatoes in a bowl. Sprinkle red pepper flakes, cumin, salt, and pepper over them. Drizzle ½ tablespoon of oil over the sweet potatoes and toss well.
3. Spread the sweet potatoes on a baking sheet without overlapping. Place on the lower rack and bake for 30-40 minutes or until cooked through. Make sure to stir them after about 15-18 minutes of baking.
4. Pour one tablespoon of oil and the lime juice into a small bowl and whisk well with a small wire whisk.
5. Add seasonings and whisk again.
6. Place sweet potatoes, onion, black beans, and cilantro in a bowl and toss well.
7. Drizzle the dressing over the salad and toss well.
8. Divide the salad onto two plates and serve.

Flying Saucers

Teach the kids to spread the mayonnaise and place the other ingredients inside the pockets

Serves: 4

Preparation time: 15 minutes

Cooking time: 0 minutes

Nutritional values per serving: 1 flying saucer

Calories: 539

Fat: 39 g

Carbohydrates: 29 g

Protein: 20 g

Ingredients:

- ¼ cup mayonnaise
- 4 pita pocket halves
- 8 thin slices bologna
- 8 thin slices of tomato

- 1 tablespoon Dijon mustard
- 4 lettuce leaves
- 4 thin slices of fully cooked ham

Directions:

1. Mix the mayonnaise and mustard in a bowl. Take a tablespoon of the mayo mixture and smear it inside the pita pockets.
2. Place a lettuce leaf in each pocket. Place two slices each of bologna and tomato in each pocket. Finally, place a slice of ham in each pocket and serve.

Frozen Banana Cereal Pops

This is a good way to involve the children at a party. Teach the children to insert the Popsicle sticks, dip the banana, and drench it.

Serves: 4

Preparation time: 15 minutes

Cooking time: 0 minutes plus freezing time

Nutritional values per serving: 1 pop

Calories: 106

Fat: 1 g

Carbohydrates: 24 g

Protein: 2 g

Ingredients:

- 6 tablespoons strawberry yogurt
- 2 medium bananas, peeled, cut into two halves crosswise
- 1 cup Fruity Pebbles cereal
- 4 wooden Popsicle sticks

Directions:

1. Put the cereal in a shallow bowl. Put the yoghurt into another shallow bowl.
2. Take one Popsicle stick and insert it into the centre of each banana piece from the cut side (up to about half).
3. Hold one Popsicle stick (along with the banana) and dip it into the yoghurt.

4. Immediately dredge it in cereal and place it on a baking sheet lined with waxed paper.
5. Repeat this process with the remaining banana pops.
6. Place in the freezer until the bananas are firm (about 2 hours) and serve.

Quick Taco Wraps

You can teach the kids to roll a taco. They can learn to build a taco. Older kids can be taught to use a hand mixer

Serves: 2

Preparation time: 15 minutes

Cooking time: 0 minutes

Nutritional values per serving: 1 taco

Calories: 533

Fat: 28 g

Carbohydrates: 48 g

Protein: 14 g

Ingredients:

- ¼ cup cream cheese, softened
- 2 tablespoons sour cream
- ¼ cup bean dip
- ¼ cup guacamole
- ½ small sweet red pepper, chopped
- ½ can (from a 2 ¼ ounce can) of sliced ripe olives, drained
- 1/8 cup canned chopped green chillies (omit for the kids)
- 1 tablespoon taco seasoning
- 2 flour tortillas (10 inches each)
- ½ small onion, chopped
- ¼ cup shredded cheddar cheese

Directions:

1. Place cream cheese in a small bowl and beat until creamy.
2. Add green chillies, taco seasoning, and sour cream until well combined.
3. Spread the tortillas on plates. Smear 2 tablespoons of bean dip over each tortilla, leaving about ½ inches from the edges.

4. Spread two tablespoons of guacamole over the bean dip. Spread the cream cheese mixture over the guacamole.
5. Scatter onion, cheese, pepper, and olives. Starting from the side closest to you, roll the taco right up to the opposite end—place with its seam side facing down.
6. Serve right away.

Kitchen Dictionary

Cooking with children is a great way to improve your bond and raise their self-esteem. Apart from this, it makes him more aware of what they are eating and encourages them to try healthy foods. Another benefit is it provides exposure to new vocabulary associated with kitchen, food, and cooking. From improving their vocabulary to increasing their interest in household chores and developing interest in the food they eat, helping your child learn kitchen vocabulary is important.

Basic kitchen work is something that all children must know before beginning to cook.

- Add: To put something with another thing. For instance, add a cup of sugar.
- Bake: A cooking technique where ingredients are cooked using dry heat, such as in the oven or air fryer.
- Boil: Heat a liquid until bubbles appear on the surface, such as bringing the water to a boil.
- Chop: Cutting something into smaller pieces. For instance, chop carrots into small pieces.

- Frying: It's a technique of cooking food in hot fat or oil to ensure the ingredients become crispy.
- Grate: The process of rubbing an ingredient on the greater to get small pieces. For instance, the recipe can say something along the lines of, "use grated cheese."
- Grill: Grilling is a technique of cooking food over Kohls or fire by placing it on a metal frame.
- Knead: This is the process of combining a dry and a wet ingredient with your hands to make a dough. For instance, kneading flour and water gives a dough.
- Mash: This is the process of crashing food by using a food mill, trainer, or mortar and pestle until it is smooth and soft.
- Marinate: This is the process of allowing an ingredient to sit in a marinate, so it soak the flavors of the marinate. Commonly used for meat or fish.
- Mix: This is the process of combining or blending ingredients into one mixture.
- Peel: The process of removing peel or skin from vegetables and fruits by using a peeler.

- Roast: The process of cooking food over a fire or in the oven is known as roasting. This is also another important cooking technique.
- Rinse: When something is washed quickly with water and without using soap, it is known as rinsing. Ensure all the ingredients you use such as fresh produce as always rinsed.
- Roll out: The process of flattening a dough by running a rolling pin over it is known as rolling out.
- Sauté: The technique of cooking something quickly using a little fat, such as oil.
- Sift: The act of passing an ingredient through a sieve to remove any large pieces is known as shifting.
- Simmer: The process of cooking at an extremely low temperature and for a prolonged period.
- Slice: The process of cutting an ingredient into flat and thin elongated pieces is known as slicing.

Recipe Journal

I hope you enjoyed this book. If you want a recipe journal that you can print and use to record your recipes; and also record your calorie intake, scan the QR code below.

Conclusion

By now, you would have realized that cooking is not only fun but easy, too! Keep cooking because it's a great way to explore and experiment with different ingredients in the kitchen. Share the delicious dishes you've whipped up with your loved ones! Keep practicing, be creative, and don't forget to have fun in the kitchen!

All the best, little chef!